Best Things
In The Worst Times

An Insider's View of World Vision

Graeme S. Irvine

BookPartners, Inc.
Wilsonville, Oregon

BookPartners, Inc.
P. O. Box 922
Wilsonville, Oregon 97070

Published in association with the Literary Agency of
Lois Curley Enterprises, San Diego, California.

To my wife Fran,
and daughters Jo and Ros.
Without their love and courage
I would have no story
to tell.

The title of this book was inspired by these words chiseled on the doorway to a parish church in Leicestershire, England:

In the year 1653
When all things sacred were throughout the nation
either demolisht or profaned,
Sir Robert Shirley Barronet
founded this church;
Whose singular praise it is
to have done the best things in the worst times
and
to have hoped them in the most calamitous.

I want this book to offer a vision of hope to all who seek a better world. Nothing would satisfy me more than to have my story become a legacy of learning for all who serve in World Vision, as well as enriching the insights of people in other organizations, churches, missions, colleges — and the wider public.

Graeme Irvine

Table of Contents

A caring man, a walk in the rain and my life is forever changed. It becomes another strand, along with a God-given vision and a humanitarian organization, in the rope which binds World Vision together.

Bob Pierce, a young evangelist in Asia, sees and responds to overwhelming needs — particularly those of children — as World Vision is shaped in post-war Korea. Ted Engstrom comes to rescue an over-extended mission. Pierce's resignation ends World Vision's "first generation" — 1950 to 1967.

World Vision branches out to Australia and New Zealand despite internal troubles. These young offices take regional initiatives and represent a new voice in World Vision.

New president Stan Mooneyham leads World Vision into a world hunger campaign and media outreach. New programs are started in Cambodia, but the door closes on Indochina amid the tragedy of war. Refugees are cared for on land and sea. World Vision returns to rekindle hope in Cambodia.

Welfare and relief are not enough in response to the scandal of poverty — lasting change requires a development approach. The decision to walk along the development path brings a major change of direction for World Vision.

World Vision enters a new era of shared vision through "internationalization" as a new course is set towards a global partnership. The ministry extends to every continent. Stan Mooneyham resigns and Ted Engstrom bridges the gap until Tom Houston comes as president in 1984.

The focus swings from Asia to Africa as the Ethiopia crisis gets world attention. The huge relief response opens the door to large scale development. Africa becomes a symbol of the human struggle against poverty, conflict and disaster.

Africa's crisis calls for a new level of international cooperation. World Vision develops closer relations with the U.N., the churches and other organizations, answers its critics, and forms alliances for urban renewal. Tom Houston resigns as president and World Vision faces internal strain.

After ten years of growth and change since internationalization, many feel a need for a clearer sense of identity and mission. A process begins that produces a set of core values, redefines the mission and frames a Covenant of Partnership.

Out of concern for social justice, World Vision becomes a more visible advocate for oppressed people. In corridors of power, in the public arena and in local communities World Vision speaks for victims of conflict, for the dignity of women and the protection of children.

While armed conflict casts its shadow of death over much of humanity, especially children, the cost of war is borne by all people. World Vision continues to work in war zones, but directs special efforts toward reducing conflict, banning land mines and working for peace.

A holistic view of the gospel is at the heart of World Vision's integrated approach to mission. Are we evangelical or ecumenical? How do we relate to the church?

World Vision's mission of transformation calls for transformation in the organization itself as it learns from its successes and failures, forms its leadership, deals with issues of accountability, and keeps its focus on serving and caring for people.

A look behind the scenes reveals the dangers, pressures and trials that staff and families face in pursuing World Vision's mission.

Entering unmapped territory in a rapidly changing world requires a new global vision, a globalization-from-below. Sustaining a vision of hope.

Foreword

Having known Graeme Irvine for twelve years, and World Vision rather longer, I take great pleasure in commending this book. I have four particular reasons for doing so.

First, the author. Graeme is a man to whom the word holy can be applied without embarrassment or fear of contradiction. In his humility, his quiet dedication and his inner simplicity, the quality of his person shows whose servant he is. Notwithstanding the jokes he tells on himself (or perhaps because of them), readers cannot but be aware that they are sharing the life journey — the faith pilgrimage — of a very special human being.

Second, the organization. World Vision has come a long way in a short time. During Graeme's period of leadership, it has changed from an enthusiastic "go-get-'em" type of operation — one that sometimes (but not always) has been brilliantly successful in impossible situations — into a mature, reflective, self-critical organization that is transforming the quality of life for hundreds of thousands of poverty stricken and war torn families throughout the world. Even more than that, World Vision has become the type of caring organization that knows it has to go on learning, experimenting and taking risks if it is to be faithful to its mandate. The scale of this reassessment of its own spirituality is a monument to Graeme's leadership; there can be no finer epitaph.

Third, the story. As the reader will soon discover, Graeme has a way with a story. He lets it speak for itself, and in this volume the reader will find some stories that will move her or him to tears. And some that will, thank God, make laughter uncontainable. World Vision is the meeting place of all kinds of people, each with his own gifts, his own joys and his own wounds. As they encounter each other in the struggle to make the world a little closer to how God intends it to be, they leave their footprints on the pages that follow. It is a privilege and a delight to walk in them.

Fourth, the message. There are many ways of reading this book and different people will read it from differing perspectives. There will be few, however, who will not be struck by the powerful way in which Graeme shares his own — and World Vision's — difficult transition from a compassionate concern for the victims of war and poverty to a well informed, strategic and often frustrating engagement with the fundamental causes of conflict and impoverishment. This shift has challenged World Vision to its roots, in both a metaphorical and a literal sense. For none of us — the sponsors or subscribers on the ground who are the literal root of World Vision — likes to recognize his individual and corporate involvement in the processes that make for war and misery. This book will help us face unflinchingly the simple but profound truth that the world will change only when we do.

In offering us this book, Graeme has, in characteristic style, set the seal on his 28 years with World Vision. Unselfishly. For others. And with a twinkle in the eye. He is truly a gift to us all. And so is his book.

Charles Elliott
Trinity Hall, Cambridge, UK
All Saints Day, 1995

Part I

How It All Started

What lies behind us and what lies before us are nothing compared with what lies within us.

– Ralph Waldo Emerson

The View From Down Under

My story runs on three tracks or pathways. One path is the vision — prophetic and God-given — that launched World Vision and propelled its global outreach. Another path is the organization that struggled, sometimes painfully, to give to the vision structural strength and direction. The other is a man, whose life has been profoundly inspired and shaped by the vision and whose career through nearly thirty years has been interwoven with the organization. I am that man.

Not that I am the only one shaped by, or in some measure who has shaped, World Vision. Founder Bob Pierce, Stan Mooneyham, Ted Engstrom and Tom Houston preceded me in the presidential chair. Each has given unique strength and color to the lengthening cords of this organization. And, of course, World Vision has been fashioned not only by its presidents, but by a multitude of men and women who have set out to help people in the most troubled parts of the earth. Today this all adds up to World Vision.

My almost 30 years inside World Vision allow me the privilege of sharing my perspective on its history and its place in the international scene. And since my Australian background influences my outlook, this perspective could be called "a view from down under."

My part of the story began when I was born into the home of Enid and Clyde Irvine in Tasmania, Australia, in July, 1931. But another day of beginning came when I was a young man just starting to work in an insurance office — a day that was to change the course of my life.

My father introduced my brother and me to Bill Clack. He had recently come to our city to reactivate the YMCA after World War II. My father and Bill had been together in a front-line Australian Air Force base in Papua-New Guinea during the war. Bill promptly invited me to join a new group he was starting the following Tuesday night. I made up my mind not to join. I did not know much about the YMCA, and anyway, I played tennis on Tuesday nights.

When Tuesday came, heavy rain came with it! No tennis. I had my head down at my desk when I was told someone wanted to see me. I looked up and there was Bill Clack, looking like Father Flanagan of Boys' Town. His hat dripped water over his face, and his overcoat was soaked. He had walked several blocks in the pouring rain to see me!

"Are you coming tonight?" he asked.

As he looked me straight in the eye with his open, caring gaze, I simply could not refuse.

"Y-Yes," I stammered.

There were three of us at the first meeting. Bill asked me if I would serve as president. As the membership grew, he said, and we got to know each other, we would have elections. One of the others was asked to be secretary and the third, treasurer. The treasurer, incidentally, collected our money and did not turn up again!

However, the club grew and became one of the most formative influences in my life. Bill Clack later led me to personal faith in Jesus Christ and set my feet on the path of my life's work. In 1954, seven years after that wet afternoon visit, I took over from him as general secretary of our local YMCA. I know he has held me in his heart and prayers ever since, and still does today. What a slender thread sometimes connects us to our destiny! A caring man, a walk in the rain, and a life is forever changed.

A GOOD ORGANIZATION — VERY RELIABLE

In 1962, when I was working with the YMCA in the city of Adelaide, South Australia, I met Bernard Barron, the director of World Vision in Canada. Bernard had come to Australia to arrange a speaking tour for a famous missionary, Gladys Aylward, and I was a member of the planning committee for her visit to Adelaide.

Gladys Aylward was a sensation! Made famous by the book, *The Small Woman* by Alan Burgess, and the movie, *The Inn of the Sixth Happiness,* with Ingrid Bergman in the starring role, Miss Aylward drew huge audiences wherever she went. In a remarkable act of courage and fortitude, she had shepherded more than 100 Chinese children in a long march to safety from invading Japanese troops. Reaching Taiwan, she continued her work among children, supported by World Vision.

From this initial contact with Bernard Barron of the Canadian office, I liked what I learned about World Vision. When I asked Gladys Aylward for her opinion, she replied in her typical no-nonsense manner, "A good organization. Very reliable."

Soon after her visit, Bernard approached me about the possibility of joining the World Vision team to open an office in Australia. I declined, believing that my work in the Australian YMCA was not finished.

When he returned in 1966 to establish the office, despite World Vision's leadership and financial difficulties at that time, Bernard knew it was the right time for World Vision in Australia. The combination of evangelism and social action, plus the forward-looking style of the organization, appealed to Australian evangelicals.

Again Bernard asked me if I would consider becoming director of the Australian office. This time I sensed a freedom to accept. With our two small daughters, my wife Fran and I moved to Melbourne. Eighteen years of work with the YMCA ended. For us the World Vision era began. It was January 1, 1968.

Though I was no stranger to humanitarian work, Bernard set about giving me my World Vision education. He had me perform tasks in every aspect of our operation — opening and answering correspondence, filing, repairing films, doing the accounts, speaking to church groups. Each day we would get a sandwich for lunch in the office and he would tell me World Vision's "tribal stories." Bob Pierce, World Vision's founder and first president, had already left, but I felt I got to know him and others in the organization through these conversations.

My orientation included three months overseas. First, I had one month in the Monrovia, California, headquarters. From there I went to Canada and then to each of the field offices, starting with Korea, where it all began. At the World Vision guest house in Seoul, I occupied the room

Bob Pierce had always used. Watching the dawn break over the great city, I wondered how many times he had looked out upon it from that very window, had wept over its suffering, prayed for its people. I felt the presence of Bob Pierce in this place more than anywhere else.

The journey of orientation included Japan, Taiwan, Hong Kong, Vietnam and Indonesia. That was about the extent of World Vision's ministry in 1968 apart from a small work in India. After meeting many of the people I had heard or read about — the pioneers of World Vision's first generation — I returned eager to take up the challenge in Australia.

OFFERING A VISION OF HOPE

Now that I have introduced my part of the story, let me return to the other two pathways — the vision and the organization.

When I think about World Vision, I recall an inscription in Old English chiseled on the doorway of the parish church at Staunton Harold in Leicestershire, England:

In the year 1653 When all things sacred were throughout the nation either demolisht or profaned, Sir Robert Shirley Barronet founded this church; Whose singular praise it is to have done the best things in the worst times and to have hoped them in the most calamitous.

"Doing the best things in the worst times" — that about sums up World Vision's philosophy. The best things may not be the obvious things. They are certainly not the easiest. Doing them in the worst times and the hardest places will stretch any person or organization to the limits of endurance and capacity. We will often fall short of our own expectations — and those of others

Yet this is the tension in which the poor and uprooted people of the world are caught up every day of their lives. Every time, for them, is the "worst time." There seems to be no "best thing." But even in the midst of poverty, violence and despair, hope can be reborn. For those who have eyes to see, the seeds of hope reside in the human heart, waiting to be recognized, released and nurtured. Hope is not merely a luxury enjoyed by the rich and secure. For most of the world's poor it is their only chance of survival.

I want this book to offer a vision of hope to all who seek a better world. In the firm belief that our source of hope is Jesus Christ, I want my telling of the World Vision story to show how the vision, the organization itself, the people in it and those it serves are changed by the transforming work of Christ.

AN ORGANIZATION IN TRANSITION

I intend the story to show that the core ministries Bob Pierce began in the 1950s — childcare, relief, evangelism and conferences to train and encourage pastors — are carried on to this day. These have, however, taken on new dimensions beginning with community development, advocacy for peace and justice and a deliberate holism of perspective and outreach.

Consequently, World Vision has been organizationally restructured to reflect its global character and to support the changing nature of its mission. These organizational developments are essential to the story.

As I recount in Chapter 2 how the vision was born, I will be glancing into a rear-view mirror to look at the earliest years of World Vision. There we will see the motivation and pivotal experiences of founder Bob Pierce. This will complete Part I, "How It All Started."

Then the story moves into World Vision's "second generation", which is where I belong. Parts II, III, IV and V describe several fundamental transitions in World Vision's pilgrimage — you could call them paradigm shifts. Part V also draws together the primary connecting threads of the journey thus far.

Let me make clear that I am not presenting a formal history of World Vision. Neither am I attempting to make this book a comprehensive record of events, people or issues. Rather, I am offering a personal perspective. I am also conveying experiences, struggles, achievements and hopes of many people with whom I have been privileged to work.

Again, I would remind my readers that I am intertwining the pathways of the story, not into a precise chronological pattern, but rather into a broadly-designed picture that covers approximately 45 years, nearly 30 of which I have been closely involved in the inner core of World Vision's development and decision-making.

At times the story will emphasize the path that I identify as the vision or mission that drives World Vision. Sometimes it will describe the organization that has framed and focused the vision. More often it will reflect my personal response, priorities and perspectives. As a whole, I trust that these three paths will present a clear and credible picture of World Vision across the years of its involvement in the suffering and hope of our afflicted planet.

Nothing would satisfy me more than to have my story become a legacy of learning for all who serve in World Vision, as well as enriching the insights of people in other organizations, churches, missions and colleges. My hope certainly includes the possibility that this book will bring fresh understanding not only to World Vision friends throughout the world, but to the wider public. I long to encourage all people who refuse to give way to despair, and who believe with me that it is better to light a candle than to curse the darkness. They may feel insignificant and remote as I was — a young man on an offshore island in an offshore continent. Doing the best things in the worst times may lead some to large responsibilities. To most people it means simply doing well what lies at hand.

To quote Bob Pierce, "Don't fail to do something just because you can't do everything."

Vision is seeing what others don't see, seeing before they see, seeing farther than they see.

— *John R. Mott*

2

Let My Heart Be Broken

"What are you going to do about it?"

He examined with alarm the bruises on the little girl's face and legs. She had been cruelly beaten. Tears streaked her face. Forlorn and homeless, she had been thrown out by her father like trash. And to learn that it was all because of him, Robert Pierce! He was shocked.

"What are you going to do about it?"

Eight words that changed Bob Pierce's life.

The young evangelist had gone to China to preach. It was his first journey outside the United States and his first encounter with another culture. Now he saw before him the result of his message in one child's life.

The place was a tiny island off China's northern coast. The year, 1947. At the invitation of veteran missionary, Tena Hoelkeboer, Pierce had gone to the mission school and told the children about Jesus and his great love for them. Excited by what she heard, little White Jade rushed home and told her family she loved Jesus. She had become a Christian. This was not good news to her father, who whipped the child and sent her away.

She went to the only person she knew who might comfort her. But Tena already had six children in her care, supported from her meager allowance.

"Well, what are you going to do about it?," Tena asked, thrusting the child into Bob Pierce's arms.

Pierce himself was only 32, with a young wife. What little money they had was used toward his ticket to China. He had only five dollars left in his pocket.

"All I have is five dollars," he said.

"That will do for now," Tena replied. "And if you will send me five dollars every month, I'll let White Jade sleep in my kitchen like my other six do. I promise to take care of her."

"I'll do it!" Pierce said.

With the passing of time the story of White Jade has become part of World Vision's folklore; many different versions having been told, even by Bob himself. What is certain is that the encounter sowed the seeds of World Vision in one man's heart.

Friends said Bob Pierce was never the same after his return to the United States. In China, and on a later mission to Korea, he saw human need on a scale beyond anything he had known. The exposure of his passionate heart to such suffering was like connecting two high-voltage terminals. He became disturbed and restless, as if a great inner struggle was going on. And indeed it was.

Bob Pierce was an evangelist, a preacher of the Christian gospel. But what was this gospel, this "good news?" Words alone, he discovered, were not necessarily good news to someone who needed food, or clothing, or shelter or medicine. As he preached, the faces of hungry children haunted him. Their cries for help stole his peace. Something was lacking in his evangelism.

He came to realize that Christian faith was more than accepting a formula. Suffering, surrendering, accepting, healing, caring and renewing were all part of the experience. He needed to give, as well as tell, the gospel. Never again could he be content with Christ's message as words alone. Looking at the world with new eyes — some might say with the eyes of Jesus — Pierce's traditional evangelical theology had acquired a new heartbeat.

As the storm clouds of war gathered over Korea, Bob Pierce became a voice in the West for Korean Christians. He wrote stories. He captured images of conflict on film. He warned of the danger to South Korea's churches. His first-hand reports moved audiences profoundly. People were eager to help. World Vision's moment had come.

An unforgettable character, Bob was the kind of man you knew would start something. And having started it, his whole being would be poured into it. That is how it was with World Vision. He stopped only long enough for the new organization to be incorporated in August 1950. He had chosen the name one night on the way home from a meeting.

Back in Korea, having somehow secured accreditation as a war correspondent, Pierce got to work amidst the appalling suffering of a country torn apart by war. There he wrote the words in the fly-leaf of his Bible that were to become his life's theme, "Let my heart be broken by the things that break the heart of God."

Bob was in his element. Impetuous by nature, daring in faith, compassionate of heart, he had found his vocation. He had set out on the great adventure. The ministry of World Vision began to take shape around the unique personality and vision of Robert Willard Pierce.

A Passion To Act

"A vision of need in Asia! The passion to act in the meeting of that need! It was almost as simple as that," wrote Vice President-at-large Paul Rees, describing World Vision's early years. "Emergency by emergency, crisis by crisis, it was a summons from Christ to act, and to act now."[1]

Action was certainly the temper of the day and Pierce called the shots. "Cut through the reasons why things can't be done," he would say and act accordingly. He went where the action was and he made things happen.

As Korea's bitter winter set in, people uprooted by the war needed shelter, food, warmth. He was there, organizing emergency aid wherever he could.

Children were the most vulnerable. Bob Pierce saw mothers and their children, an endless stream of humanity strung out along the freezing, wind-swept roads. Their men were somewhere fighting, perhaps dead. Carrying a few belongings in little bundles, women and children struggled on, thinking only of survival.

Many did not survive. They fell by the roadside, overcome by fatigue, exposure, hunger. Often a child would be found, huddled beside the prone figure of its mother. "Mummy, wake up. Please wake up." But this was the long sleep of death, from which there was no waking. A passer-

1. Declaration of Internationalization, 1978.

by would gather up the child and move on. Korea's generation of orphans increased daily. The question was how to care for them.

Christians cared — Korean Christians, simple people with few resources, but with big hearts. These people, mainly women, took in the orphans, sharing their homes, their food, their love. Sometimes twenty or thirty children would be crowded into one tiny house. These benefactors gave all they had, but they needed help. That's where World Vision came in.

Just as Bob Pierce had given Tena Hoelkeboer five dollars each month to care for White Jade in China, so he invited North American Christians to support Korean orphans. The donors were called sponsors, and they were linked with a particular child whose photograph they received and with whom they could correspond. This sponsoring program translated need into personal terms. It reminded people that the poor were not statistics, that they had faces, names, feelings, hopes and dreams.

The churches of the south were a particular target during the Korean War. Pastors were tortured by the communist invaders, many executed. Church buildings were destroyed, congregations scattered. As peace returned, so too came the task of recovery and renewal.

One day a pastor's widow came to Bob Pierce. She had seen her husband murdered. Out of her own grief she felt the need for a message of hope to the church. Taking off her wedding ring, she gave it to Bob. "This is the only thing of value I have," she said. "Please use it to start a fund to bring the pastors together for encouragement."

From this precious seed the pastors' conference ministry of World Vision grew, starting in Korea with that first conference of 1953. Back in the U.S. and Canada, Bob

Pierce inspired a new and urgent missionary vision. Through the decade of the 1950s it was non-stop action for him and the burgeoning World Vision. "If you are ever going to do anything for Asia, do it now!" was his plea.

Underlining his sense of urgency, he pioneered the use of documentary film to report from crisis areas, often shooting the film himself. The resulting footage was used to move American audiences to act and to act immediately. It was said that if you went where Bob Pierce was speaking, you had better leave your wallet or purse at home. His appeal for action was irresistible.

In all of his non-stop travels and fund raising, Pierce never ceased to be an evangelist. His was the evangelism of deed and word. "You have to earn the right to be heard," he would say again and again. He did earn the right and he spoke the Word. The message of Jesus Christ was constantly on his lips, just as the compassion of Jesus filled his heart.

Thus the ministry of World Vision was fashioned, not in some quiet study, but in the heat of action. An early statement of purpose put it in a nutshell; "World Vision is a missionary service organization meeting emergency needs in crisis areas of the world through existing evangelical agencies."

Five "basic objectives" described the scope of its activities: 1) Christian social welfare, 2) emergency aid, 3) evangelistic outreach, 4) Christian leadership development and 5) missionary challenge.

There was something about this concise statement that fired the imagination. Here was faith in action! The idea had legs, and World Vision quickly pushed out the boundaries to other emergencies.

AS SIMPLE AS THAT

The story goes that Bob Pierce once went to an airline counter and said, "May I have a ticket please?"

"Yes, sir," said the clerk. "Where to?"

"Anywhere," replied Bob.

Not a true story, but it makes the point that World Vision's first president always seemed to be going somewhere.

From Korea the ministry extended to Hong Kong, with its enormous influx of refugees from Mao Tse Tung's China. Indonesia, Taiwan, India, Japan became part of the World Vision map. The approach to this expanding work was simple. Bob Pierce had an uncanny knack of spotting the servants of Jesus Christ working in out-of-the-way places, doing the kinds of things that expressed World Vision's objectives. He found Lillian Dickson working among the lepers of Taiwan, Gladys Donnithorne in Hong Kong's Walled City, Dr. Howard Moffett's medical outreach in Korea. Many were veteran missionaries. Others were national church leaders like Dr. Han Kyung Chik. They were colorful people, heroes and heroines of the faith. Among them Bob Pierce was a legend. He encouraged them, supported them, prayed with them, believed in them, loved them. He told their stories in person, on radio and on film.

In the United States World Vision had all the excitement of a young organization. It throbbed with life. The first office staff worked for almost nothing on borrowed desks in tiny offices. They were part of something new and robust; personally involved and part of it all. The same spirit went with them when World Vision moved to California from Portland, Oregon in 1956. An office was opened in Canada in 1954 and incorporated as a separate national entity in 1961. Canadians responded to the growing ministry as generously as their U.S. neighbors.

As Vietnam's ugly war took its toll of suffering, World Vision was once again on the scene. Here the program took a subtle but significant change of direction. Instead of working through existing channels, World Vision became increasingly operational. Refugee schools were started, with Vietnamese teachers recruited and trained by World Vision. Housing was provided for displaced people. Amputees were assisted with wheelchairs and crutches. Relief supplies were distributed. World Vision even set up its own bakery to make high protein biscuits.

In the early years the organizational style was simple. Vice President Paul Rees characterized it this way: "No long-range planning. No elaborate mechanisms of administration."[2] Anyone looking at World Vision would see an organization that was action-oriented, centered around Bob Pierce himself, strongly evangelical, innovative and progressive.

As with most things, there was another side to the coin. These apparent strengths had corresponding weaknesses: instability, dependent on the ideas and personality of one person, narrow relationships and limited international perspective.

Despite the desire of everyone for simplicity, working among the poor and afflicted in crisis areas of the world and sustained by voluntary giving was not as simple as it sounds. Pierce was wise enough to recognize this. Turning to a Youth for Christ friend of earlier days, he appealed to Ted Engstrom for help to get organized. Ted's

2. Declaration of Internationalization, 1978.

coming in 1963 as executive vice president was providential, as events soon proved.

THE END OF THE BEGINNING

By the middle of its second decade, World Vision was in trouble. Money was short. Bob Pierce was ill. His long and frequent absences imposed unbearable stress on his marriage and family. There was growing tension between Bob and his board. He resisted the changes that were needed to create a more responsible administration. He accused his closest colleagues of betrayal. Eventually it became clear to him and to the board of directors that he should resign.

With his resignation in October 1967, the pioneering years came to an end. The critical transition to the second generation began. Ted Engstrom, who had stalwartly maintained stability during the painful closing years of Pierce's leadership, held on to guide the organization through the crosscurrents of change.

The departure of a founder-leader is always difficult. His was the vision and energy that gave birth to the new enterprise. His personality molded it, his ideas inspired it. Unique loyalties tend to build around the exceptional character of the founder-leader. A mystique evolves that becomes part of the folklore of the organization.

At the same time the founder tends to develop a proprietary ownership of the organization, as did Bob Pierce. Any honest criticism is often interpreted as a breach of loyalty.

No organization can afford to ignore its history; neither can it afford to be chained to it. A sense of history preserves continuity. It reminds those who come later that they have entered into the labors of others. History becomes a negative factor when it blinds people to the ongoing journey of an organization and the process of change that is necessary for growth in size, as well as in maturity.

Jesus said to his disciples, "I have much more to say to you, more than you can now bear. But when the Spirit of truth comes, he will guide you into all truth" (John 16:12,13). Those who were with Jesus had moments of great insight and faith. There were other times of ignorance and folly. This is true of all people and their institutions. We can honor our history without becoming enslaved by it.

I met Bob personally on several occasions after his resignation and travelled with him once to Vietnam. He was a bitter man, critical of former colleagues and the new leadership of World Vision. He could not accept any way of doing things other than his own. Near the end of his life this spirit of bitterness diminished and he came to a place of reconciliation in some important relationships.

Without Bob Pierce World Vision would probably not have been born. It is equally true, in my opinion, that with him it probably would not have survived.

Part II

From Welfare To Development

An opportunity to serve, a challenge, a faith step, living in hope.

— Ruth Vicente, World Vision Mexico

3

New Kids On The Block

"This is not the right time."

When Bernard Barron, the director of World Vision in Canada, had proposed launching the new office in Australia in 1966, the executive mood was one of caution. After all, times were bad. World Vision was struggling for survival.

Ted Engstrom, however, had been infected with the visionary qualities of World Vision's founder. He saw the opportunity more clearly than the risk. He gave the green light to Bernard and agreed to provide start-up funds for the new venture, which was how I found myself at the helm of a frail but promising boat, "World Vision Australia," on its maiden voyage.

FOR THE POOR

Soon after Bernard's departure, I had occasion to visit Sydney. I was feeling the weight of all that lay ahead.

Finding myself near Wesley Chapel in the heart of Sydney's business district, I went in. As I closed the doors on the roar of traffic and the rush of hurrying crowds, the little chapel became an oasis of peace.

It had been like that nearly twenty years earlier when I last visited the chapel. I was a student then, out of work and out of money. In the quietness of prayer, God had renewed my confidence. I remembered seeing a metal collection box near the door that day as I left, engraved, "For the poor." On impulse, I had emptied my pocket of my last few coins. With only a train ticket to my name, I stepped out into the street with a light heart, to discover a job offer waiting for me on my return to college. It was a lesson in faith.

Now I knelt again in the silence. I had a vision of the vast island-continent of Australia. I saw in my imagination its 12 million people. I felt the youthful energy of the country, its fierce belief in a "fair go" for all, its emerging place in the modern world. I knew in that moment World Vision had a significant future in Australia. A great sense of peace and assurance flooded my soul.

Once again I left the chapel with a spring in my step, and yes, there it was! The same box, "For the poor." This time I felt compelled, not only to give coins, but to pour out all the energy and vision of which I was capable for the world's poor. God had opened a door of opportunity beyond my imagining.

Making World Vision A Household Word

We had a small office in Melbourne, with three enthusiastic staff members. Fran and the children helped me fold, stuff and stamp the first appeal letter on our living-room table. We sent the letter out with our prayers. The girls would come with me as week-by-week I screened World Vision films in churches. They got to know the commentaries by heart.

I felt it was important to strengthen World Vision's connection with the churches, not only for promotion, but as an act of accountability. I once asked Paul Rees for his advice on this point. "World Vision is sometimes seen by the churches as a 'shadowy' organization," he said. "They will judge World Vision by what they see in you." I took him seriously and sought every opportunity of meeting in person with church congregations as well as individual ministers and leaders.

One of World Vision's strengths was the way in which human need took on real flesh and blood. I was once speaking to a church youth group that had decided to sponsor a child. A young man in the group exclaimed, "When I go home and tell my mother I'm a dad she'll kill me!"

Our aim was not to glorify the organization, but to offer it as a window through which people could see the reality of world need and respond in a personal way. The donor could sponsor a child, provide a small home for a real refugee family, help support a national Christian worker by name.

We approached the Australian public on a broad front through the news media as well as in the churches. This was more easily said than done, because the media looked for stories to report rather than causes to support. Help was obtained from an experienced journalist, whom I engaged on a consulting basis to develop strategies and produce material for media use. Later, the son of one of our original sponsors joined the team as communications director. Creative, provocative and stimulating, David Longe's objective was "to make World Vision a household word." He saw that happen in Australia and New Zealand before his untimely death in 1983.

We established a volunteer network in the major cities, so that people could become involved personally. In one of our first projects, volunteers assembled hundreds of thousands of Vietkits. These little packages of relief supplies were of three types: hygiene kits, school kits and sewing kits. World Vision provided plastic bags and shipping. The volunteers furnished the contents as specified and packed the kits, which we sent to Vietnam for use in refugee schools and hospitals.

The work grew by leaps and bounds, doubling in volume every year. Soon we had to find larger office space, which we continued to expand as the response from Australians multiplied.

WE MUST DO SOMETHING

One day we received a letter from Dorothy Engstrom, wife of Executive Vice President Ted Engstrom. Dorothy had been to Vietnam, where she saw the heartbreak of abandoned babies in overcrowded, under-staffed institutions. No one seemed to care about them. Many would lie crying for hours with no response. As a result, these infants suffered severe physical and emotional deprivation. Dorothy's impassioned letter touched my wife's heart. "We must do something," she said. How many times would I hear those words from her in the years ahead. Many initiatives I have taken owe their birth to Fran's sensitive spirit. She sees and listens with the eyes and ears of the heart.

We did do something — the New Life Babies' Home, fully funded by Australia. Sydney pediatric nurse, Joan Potter, was the first director. She recruited Vietnamese care-givers to be with the children, play with them, talk to them and, touch them, in a new approach to addressing infant deprivation. Together they nursed and loved hundreds of children back to life. Many children were adopted by Vietnamese families. Others were adopted overseas. While not advocating inter-country adoption as the best solution for these children, World Vision helped open Australia's doors for foreign adoption and arranged the first adoption of a Vietnamese child by Australian parents.

Across The Tasman Sea

Some people have the mistaken idea that Australia and New Zealand are one country. Try telling that to a New Zealander! Not only are the two countries separated by the wide and stormy Tasman Sea, but there are distinct historical and cultural differences, despite our geographic proximity and a natural affinity between our two peoples.

Until 1971, a small number of sponsors and donors in New Zealand had been assisted by an honorary representative, Arthur Skeels, as an extension of World Vision Australia. However, a planned tour by the World Vision Korean Children's Choir to Australia and New Zealand provided the perfect opportunity to launch a full-fledged ministry in our neighbor country.

The choir, made up of 24 girls and eight boys, was world-class. Reviewers often compared favorably the quality of their voices and the precision of their presentation to the better-known Vienna Boys' Choir. Several of the children were orphans. Most came from poor families. All were sponsored through the World Vision childcare program. They saw themselves not only as musicians, but as representatives of the world's children, especially those in the so-called Third World.

I invited a young man from the Adelaide YMCA to join our staff as the tour organizer. In the 18 months before the tour, Geoff Renner went to every town and city they would visit. He organized volunteer committees in each center to promote the concerts, plan hospitality and make all local arrangements. The committees did a great job, ensuring the financial success of the tour and putting World Vision on the map in every major center in the two countries.

From the moment these gifted and beautiful children stepped off the plane in Perth until they left from Darwin three months later, I had the privilege of traveling with them and presenting them to packed concert audiences.

Part of each concert program was a violin solo by a remarkable 14-year-old, Kim Young Keun. The night before we left Australia for New Zealand, Young Keun's old violin started to give trouble. He was sure it would not last the tour. That night we gave a concert in Brisbane, broadcast internationally by Radio Australia. During the interval I shared Young Keun's problem with the audience and appealed for a replacement violin.

It happened that the technician handling the radio broadcast was a widower, whose wife had been a member of the Brisbane Symphony Orchestra. Since her death the previous year, he had kept her magnificent instrument. He did not want to sell it, but was at a loss what to do. He could not contain his excitement when he heard my appeal! We were able to announce to the audience that he would present it to our young violinist as a living memorial to his wife. The chair of the Australian World Vision Board, Robert Coles, provided a scholarship for Young Keun's continuing study of the violin with maestro Jascha Heifetz.

The New Zealand public welcomed the choir with the same enthusiasm as the Australians. Professional critics acclaimed the performances, while the media gave enormous coverage to World Vision's ministry. Even more important, the local committees in New Zealand formed a nucleus of supporters who later became a model for World Vision volunteer networks all over the world.

The children themselves were a delight to be with. Their individual stories gave living evidence of the vision of hope that is at the heart of World Vision.

Take the case of the youngest choir member, Oh Mee Soon, who had her ninth birthday during the tour. As a tiny baby, she had been left wrapped in a parcel in the city of Taegu. Miraculously, a welfare worker on the way home from work heard her cry. Gathering up the bundle, he hurried through the snow to a nearby World Vision-supported babies' home. The superintendent, Mrs. Oh, took the child in her arms and gently brought strength and life back. She named the child Mee Soon, meaning "beautiful," and gave the little stranger her own family name.

As Mee Soon grew older, her lovely singing voice developed and she auditioned for the famous choir. After her selection, she went to live and study at the World Vision Music Institute in Seoul. The journey to Australia and New Zealand was her first with the choir.

Just before intermission at each concert, I would sit with the children to interview one or two. Though they spoke no English, they knew the questions I would ask and had rehearsed their answers. Eventually Mee Soon's turn came.

Sitting beside her with my microphone, I asked, "What is your favorite verse in the Bible, Mee Soon?"

In her gentle voice, carried to a hushed audience of 3,000 people, Mee Soon quoted the 23rd Psalm. "The Lord is my shepherd, I shall not want."

Here was one of the lost lambs Jesus spoke about in Matthew 18. Through the love of Korean Christians she had been found and tenderly restored to life. Now she trusted in the Good Shepherd, who laid down his life for the sheep.

Fran and I took a special interest in Mee Soon over the years, her birth date being the same as that of our younger daughter. Most recently we were in her apartment in Seoul, where she now lives with her husband, small daughter, Gee Hei, and baby son. We inaugurated World Vision of New Zealand to coincide with the choir visit. Geoff Renner agreed to stay on as executive director, bringing to the task the same entrepreneurial energy that made the choir tour such a success. As in Australia, progress was rapid. Within two years the new entity was fully self-supporting under its own Board of Directors. Today World Vision of New Zealand has the highest per capita giving of any country in the World Vision family.

MAKING HISTORY IN PAPUA-NEW GUINEA

I never knew what the day's mail would bring. One day I opened an interesting looking letter from Papua-New Guinea, Australia's Trust Territory to the north. Intriguing! Who could be writing from there?

"Would World Vision consider conducting a Pastors' Conference for the young churches of Papua-New Guinea and the Solomon Islands?" the letter asked. This was a job for Vice President-at-large Dr. Paul Rees, I thought, and sent the letter to him. No, it was a job for me, he responded, asking me to meet with church leaders, I was to try to widen the invitation, involve all the churches and get a committee organized. I had not expected that; it's called "trust."

I began by consulting with church leaders of all denominations and with both the Evangelical Alliance and the Melanesian Council of Churches. I also met with a number of missionary leaders. I noted with interest the open, accepting attitude of national church leaders like Bishop Simon Gaius of the United Church, or Bishop Zurewe of the Lutheran Church, compared to the more cautious and sometimes cynical reaction of missionary leaders. Their pessimism was obvious especially when I said our aim was to have the conference planned and conducted by national leaders.

One missionary executive laughed at this notion. "There's no way they can do that," he scoffed. My observation of the missionary's negative attitude was not intended to demean them. Missionaries and their families have made colossal sacrifices for the sake of the gospel, especially in the harsh Papua-New Guinea environment. Sometimes World Vision may have appeared to be a Johnny-come-lately, reaping the fruit of generations of missionary endeavor. I salute those whose labors we have entered into. But mission administrators, who are often far removed from field realities, may adopt a patronizing attitude, treating indigenous leaders like children, ignoring the natural wisdom they bring to the ministry of Christ.

The Lutheran Church declined to participate, a decision reached in the United States, I was told. This was disappointing, since about one third of all Christians in New Guinea were Lutheran. We felt it was important to include them. A group of national church leaders, representing nearly all the churches, formed themselves into a committee to take the issue of the conference in hand. Eventually they extended a unanimous invitation to World Vision and the planning went ahead, led by the indigenous group. Anglican minister John Key, based in Port Moresby, played an important role behind the scenes.

The conference was historic — the first time pastors had met across such broad denominational lines. Although the Roman Catholic Church declined to participate, the Archbishop gave a moving opening address.

One beautiful scene stands out in my mind. A pastor from a conservative group in one part of the country embraced a priest from the Anglican Church in another part. The two were completely different, ecclesiastically. "Forgive me, my brother," said one. "I thought we were the only true Christians." This spirit of reconciliation and unity has been a typical outcome of these conferences.

World Vision Australia accepted responsibility for coordinating four conferences — two in Papua-New Guinea, one in the New Hebrides (now Vanuatu), and one for Australian aboriginal Christian leaders, both men and women. Ugandan church leader Festo Kivengere was a key speaker in three of these conferences. His insightful approach was a revelation to many, especially the Australian Aborigines. "You don't have to be less of an Aborigine to be a Christian," he declared. "Christ makes you a more authentic Aborigine."

NO TURNING BACK

I have described the early years of World Vision Australia at length because that is where my own experience was. Colleagues in every country could give a similar account of their successes and failures. Their struggles and joys were just as real as ours in Australia. In time, World Vision put down roots in several countries of Europe. Each one has its own story of endeavor, of generous giving, of dedicated work by staff and boards and contribution to the larger mission of World Vision.

Pioneering is exciting work! In Australia and New Zealand we broke new ground. Every day seemed to bring new opportunities and challenges, opening every envelope was like getting a letter from a member of the family. Our staff loved the organization and believed profoundly in its mission. We took risks, tried new ideas, expanded the vision. World Vision's senior international leadership trusted us with regional and international initiatives. We were the new kids on the block, but we were given the dignity of participation.

As the Australian and New Zealand programs grew, something else was starting to happen in the larger World Vision family. Ours was a new voice, one that was not comfortable to all. One executive told me that Australia was merely "an out-station for collecting funds"!

That is not the way we saw it. We were looking for authentic participation in policy and decision-making, a say in the affairs of the organization.

At an international conference in Asia I had expressed an opinion on some policy issues. This led to a special meeting to take me to task for what was seen as a critical attitude. "Don't you trust us?" I was asked. Apparently open debate was not welcome, at least by some. Others recognized in the different voice from Down Under a movement toward global partnership that would bring historic change to World Vision in the 1970s. There was no turning back.

It is folly to wait for a better time, a more suitable place or a more favorable circumstance. Caring is for now, because now is the only time we have. If not now, when? If not here, where? If not us, who?

— Stan Mooneyham

4

Caring Can't Wait

T he tall American stood up and extended his hand as
I approached. His grip was firm, his smile
warm. "You must be Graeme Irvine," he said. "I'm
Stan Mooneyham. Please join us." His hand indicated the
group seated at a patio table in the cool of the tropical
evening. "Sit down. I'll introduce you later to each of these
friends."

He was with a group of Christian leaders, hearing
their views on the state of the church in Indonesia.
Obviously he was a good listener and a strategic thinker.

This first encounter was just before his appointment
to the World Vision presidency. When I met him a year later
in Australia he had been appointed president, but had not
yet taken office. My first impression was confirmed as we
discussed ideas about World Vision. I felt the energy and
drive of the man. Here was someone who liked to get things
done. I looked forward to working with him.

In July 1969 W. Stanley Mooneyham became World Vision's second president. And with the new president, a new direction began.

Stan allowed himself a year or so to absorb the World Vision culture and get to know the people. By then we were into the 1970s, a decade in which he would be the dominant figure in World Vision. It was also a decade that would bring the two of us into a close working relationship.

Though I was far removed in Australia from World Vision's center of gravity in California, Stan took the trouble to keep me in touch with events. He would phone from somewhere in the world to tell me about an idea he was working on or to share a recent experience. He did not try to dictate the direction of World Vision in Australia or impose his ideas. I had the feeling of being a colleague, a trusted partner. I joined him on several field survey trips where he welcomed my ideas and I, in turn, got to know him better. Occasionally he asked me to represent him at some event.

WHAT DO YOU SAY TO A HUNGRY WORLD?

Stan Mooneyham had a larger-than-life quality. He saw everything on a giant screen, with quadrophonic sound. "If you are going to make a mistake," he would say, "make it a big one!" Better, however, to make it a big success!

Stan was searching for a bold initiative that would inject new vision and energy into the organization. He found it in the growing problem of world hunger. He had also been a journalist early in his career. He knew the power of the media and wanted to harness it for World Vision's mission.

Bringing the two ideas together, he launched a campaign against world hunger, using television extensively in the United States to present special programs. The results were dramatic as World Vision entered the television era.

Stan's well-researched book, *What Do You Say to a Hungry World?* got good reviews as a serious contribution to an understanding of the issue. He enlisted prominent people like U.S. Senator Mark Hatfield to sponsor hunger events. It was natural that this kind of emphasis on hunger would take us toward Africa and point us in the direction of development in the years to come.

By the early 1970s World Vision had turned the corner financially. We were known by a wider public through television and had engaged the attention of recognized development specialists like Dean Freudenberger of the School of Theology in Claremont, California.

A LOVE AFFAIR WITH CAMBODIA

While traveling in Asia early in his presidency, Stan learned that the small country of Cambodia was in the grip of a malaria epidemic. He filled his suitcase with medicine and headed for Phnom Penh, handing over the medicine to Dr. Mi Samedi of the Cambodian Red Cross. This began what Stan called his "love affair with Cambodia," which endured till the end of his life.

A few months later, as Cambodia sank deeper into war, Stan loaded a truck with relief supplies in Saigon and took it across the border to Phnom Penh through the war zone, an act as symbolic as it was daring. The small Protestant church, fruit of the Christian and Missionary Alliance ministry, welcomed World Vision's response in support of their own valiant efforts to serve Phnom Penh's swelling refugee population.

This early relief work opened a window of opportunity for an evangelistic outreach sponsored by the church.

As he prepared for this, Stan found in Cambodian folklore a cultural parallel with the message of the Cross. This helped him bridge the cultural gap that so often leads to an assumption that Christianity is a Western religion. It was a strategic moment, strengthening the young church for the trial yet to come.

Part of Stan Mooneyham's dream for Cambodia was a Christian Children's Hospital. Health care was simply not available to the poor and as always, children were the most vulnerable. Plans were drawn up and a proposal put to the World Vision Board. To his great disappointment they turned it down. I had been to Cambodia many times and saw the appalling condition of the hospitals. Streams of refugees pouring into Phnom Penh overwhelmed the few medical resources.

World Vision had no office in Cambodia. Again the nagging imperative, something must be done! Why not start a mobile medical program instead of the hospital? You could treat more people that way and take the treatment to where people lived. World Vision Australia and New Zealand put up the proposal, offering to organize, staff and fund the program. Stan agreed.

First we needed a doctor to take charge. Not any doctor, but one medically competent for the kinds of problems we would encounter and able to organize and lead under war conditions. We turned to one of our childcare sponsors, Dr. Penelope Key, sister of John Key, who had worked with me on the Papua-New Guinea Pastors' Conference. A phone call to the Island of Skye, Scotland, connected me with Pene (pronounced "Penny"). Her "Yes, I'll do it," reminded me of Bob Pierce's response to Tena Hoelkeboer way back in 1947.

Pene began with two nurse volunteers from Melbourne. Recruiting the nurses brought some interesting people to light. One day our receptionist warned me that an elderly lady insisted on seeing me. She was an applicant for the Cambodia nursing team.

"I know what you are going to say, young man," she began as she was admitted to my office. "You think I'm too old. Let me tell you I do twenty press-ups every day!"

At seventy years of age that is some achievement. I would have loved to take her because of her determination. However, we really needed younger nurses with specialized training for the Cambodia job. Reluctantly, I had to decline.

With the team on its way, we organized gifts of medicines and supplies from Australian manufacturers. Within a week Pene was on the phone. "We don't need more medicine," she said. "We need food — shiploads of food." She had found widespread malnutrition among the children. Dealing with that was the top priority. It was not a job to be attempted by our small team alone. So Pene invited UNICEF, Catholic Relief Services and the Red Cross to join with World Vision in a shared nutrition program for children. In addition, we ran clinics in the major refugee centers.

NO TIME FOR TEARS

During a 1974 visit, I went to one of these clinics near the partially-built Cambodiana Hotel. The great concrete shell of the hotel served as a makeshift home for several thousand refugees. Most of them were packed into the basement, camping on the earth floor, which flooded every time it rained. Dark, damp and dismal, this was typical of the miserable life of the refugee. A few hundred yards away stood a little hut where Pene and her team worked. When I arrived, I found about 300 people waiting outside for treatment. Mothers with babies, small children coughing and dirty, old people hanging onto life — they were all jammed around the one small door.

I managed to get through somehow and reached the consulting room, where I stepped into the middle of an emergency. A little boy lay on the table, critically ill from bronchial pneumonia. He struggled for breath with loud wheezing gasps as Pene did everything in her power to save him.

Taking a tube, she inserted it into the boy's throat and sucked out the phlegm, spitting it into a bowl. I marvelled at her total commitment to this little scrap of humanity, ignoring the risk to herself. As a last resort she injected adrenaline into the boy's heart, but as I held his hand, his breathing stopped altogether and he was gone. The struggle was over.

There was no time for tears; they would come later. The mother was in the room with us, but I could hardly bear to look at her. Gently taking the boy in her arms, Pene carried him to one of her assistants.

"Go with the mother," she said. "Stay with her through the day."

Other patients were waiting. The work had to go on. But later that night, as we gathered in the team house, we wept and prayed and shared the grief we felt. Someone once said to me, "There are so many children in the world and they face such a miserable life. Wouldn't it be kinder to let them die?" She was a caring person, absolutely sincere. But we could only say that about someone else's child. To that Cambodian mother, her child was beyond price and Pene Key had fought as valiantly and skillfully for his life in that remote dispensary as she would have in any of the world's greatest hospitals.

The next day I had to leave for Australia. I found myself sitting next to a doctor returning from a conference of gynecologists. Once we had settled in our seats and were off the ground, I started to tell him about our work in Cambodia, with the experience of yesterday so fresh in my mind. In the middle of my story, a voice came from the speaker overhead.

"Is there a doctor on board, please? We have an emergency."

"Sounds like me," he said, and hurried off.

An hour later he returned to tell me he had delivered a baby boy! When the birth was announced everyone broke into clapping and cheering. The news reached Sydney ahead of us and we were greeted by the media in full force. Our new arrival was on the front page next day. Qantas Airways would give diapers. Johnson and Johnson donated a year's supply of baby products.

I could not help but contrast our high-flying birth with the grief of a mother in Cambodia. One child is born amid public fanfare; 5,000 miles away another dies in obscurity; uprooted, with no home, no grave, no hope. The message for me was: *you can't celebrate life in one part of the world, while ignoring suffering in another.* We are one human family, sharing a common humanity.

The Cambodia medical program, like the pastors' conferences, was another example of World Vision's emerging international partnership at work. It also illustrated the principle of looking for alternative solutions to a major problem. A few months after the Australian initiative, World Vision opened an office in Phnom Penh and the responsibility was transferred from Australia to the field leadership. At the height of the program, nearly 30,000 people were being treated every month, mainly women and children. A senior UNICEF official described it as one of the most effective programs he had seen.

Penelope Key was honored by Britain's Queen Elizabeth II for her remarkable work in Cambodia. The last time I met her, twenty years later she was back in Cambodia assessing health needs on behalf of the British Government. That's commitment!

The refugee medical program in Cambodia revealed how badly a children's hospital was needed, a dream that Stan Mooneyham refused to give up. It was a dream shared by others as well, notably the late Winston Weaver, a member of the U.S. Board of Directors of World Vision. Winston had shared Stan's disappointment about the earlier decision, and had gone back to the drawing board to develop a simpler design, working with John Calder, chair of World Vision New Zealand. Together they came up with a new plan, more suited to the Cambodian context and far less expensive.

Work went ahead on land made available at no charge by the Phnom Penh authorities, an excellent site directly opposite the University Medical School, in which Dr. Penelope Key had found time to teach. The new facility was completed, equipped, staffed and about to commence its long-awaited work of healing when disaster struck. The Khmer Rouge stormed into Phnom Penh, bringing with them the murderous plan they would unleash on an unsuspecting people. Once again the dream blew up in our faces.

GOD'S PLAN FOR US

One August night in 1974, Stan Mooneyham called me in Melbourne. He asked if I would consider moving to California to lead World Vision's field operations.

"Are you open to it?" he said, after we had discussed some of the issues.

"Yes," I replied. "I couldn't be a servant of Jesus Christ if I were not willing to consider it."

Fran and I talked it over with our friends, David and Elizabeth Bill. David had been our first World Vision volunteer helper in Australia. We felt the excitement of the challenge and all that it represented. I was to attend a meeting the following week in California, so Stan suggested Fran come with me to assess the implications for the family. Our two daughters had just left for a holiday with their grandmother in Sydney, so we decided to get all the information before broaching the subject with them.

On our return, we talked, we prayed, we sought direction. One morning at breakfast, someone said, "I think it's God's plan for us." That seemed to sum it up. So, as we began our eighth year with World Vision, we headed for California.

CRISIS IN INDOCHINA

Almost at once a major crisis faced the organization. One third of all our ministry was in Vietnam, Cambodia and Laos, where the population on both sides of the Indochina conflict suffered terribly. In Vietnam, the balance was moving in favor of the North. Our director in Vietnam, Canadian Don Scott, estimated that the South would not hold out for more than two years. Stan and I thought it would be longer. It proved to be less than two months!

In Cambodia the Khmer Rouge pressed in on Phnom Penh. The same story came from Laos, where the Pathet Lao were gaining the upper hand. I later had a brush with them at gunpoint when they occupied our Vientiane office.

Stan and I decided to go together to Indochina to confer with our people on the ground. The situation grew worse daily and by the time we arrived, our staff members were facing certain evacuation. Cambodia was the most urgent. The Khmer Rouge had the airport and perimeter of Phnom Penh under constant rocket attack. We loaded a chartered C-46 aircraft with medical supplies and food in Bangkok to support the remaining staff, who were attempting to keep the program going. The plane was a patched-up remnant flown by an ex-air force, devil-may-care type who was the only person we could find crazy enough to do the mission.

Our plan was to leave the supplies and evacuate the youngest and most vulnerable infants from our nutrition center. By means of radio, we arranged for them to be brought to the Phnom Penh airport in baskets, which we would tie down to the floor of the plane. Pene Key agreed to come with us, a brave decision considering the extreme danger she had endured for months before her evacuation the previous day.

Our pilot, an experienced war veteran, kept the aircraft low as we approached Phnom Penh. Puffs of white smoke were visible long before we could make out the actual explosions of rockets on the airport and the smoke from the fires they had started. It was a tense moment, but once we landed, our thoughts were occupied with unloading the plane and getting the babies aboard — all twenty-three of them. Our deputy director for Cambodia, Minh Thien

Voan, was there to direct the action. Stan urged him to come with us. He refused.

"I must stay with the work and with the church," he said. "But please take my wife and children." He could not be persuaded to leave.

Several times we were forced to hit the ground as rockets fell near us. We were wearing helmets and flak jackets, but they are poor protection from shrapnel.

Soon we had the babies securely anchored in their baskets. We were ready to leave, but Voan's wife and children had not arrived. It was too dangerous to wait with our precious cargo. Our pilot started one engine. Then he tried the other, but it would not start! Again and again he pulled the starter without result. We knew we were exposed to danger, like a sitting duck. Suddenly, a van sped to the side of the plane and Voan's family hurried aboard. Almost in the same instant the motor fired and we began to taxi to the runway.

I helped feed the babies on the flight to Bangkok, holding one in each arm. The drone of the engines was a noisy lullaby, but we all relaxed as each passing minute took us closer to security and a safe haven in Thailand. There we had some difficulty with immigration, but we were able to get the babies through and settle them in a missionary house, where they were safe and cared for pending adoption. At the U.S. end, World Vision had been busy coordinating with Family Ministries adoption agency and arranging for the reception of the children.

One baby boy was adopted by a member of World Vision's U.S. staff, Marty Lonsdale and his wife, Karen. Karen and Marty described their decision to adopt an Asian child as "overwhelmingly positive." They understood the probability of physical and emotional damage suffered by these infant survivors. But they trusted God and knew their decision was right.

The most painful part of the process was totally unexpected. After they received baby Srin from Family Ministries, a court action by a disappointed applicant challenged the validity of all the adoptions on the grounds that the policy of placing children only with Christian families violated the rights of the children. The court ruled against Family Ministries and all the adoptions were ruled invalid. It was a moment of heartbreak for parents who had already given months of loving care to the children, now part of their family life. The Los Angeles Department of Adoptions was directed to review each case and decide on placement. The good news was that the department confirmed every one of the adoptions, commending the quality of the homes chosen! Eighteen months of uncertainty were over.

Srin was a very sick baby when he was brought to the World Vision Nutrition Center just before the evacuation. He was weak from malnutrition and had suffered from high fever and measles during the first months of his life. After his adoption by the Lonsdales he continued to have chronic bouts of diarrhea, allergies and bronchial problems. Karen and Marty loved him back to life, naming him Nathan, "gift of God." His Cambodian name, Srin, became his middle name.

Today Nathan is a healthy, well-adjusted young man and a fine track athlete. He is in his second year at college with a good future ahead. He would not have survived one week in Pol Pot's Cambodia.

Two days after the evacuation of the children the Khmer Rouge entered Phnom Penh and the reign of terror began. No one expected the insane genocide that followed.

We learned much later that Minh Voan and many others of our staff were among the victims.

Vietnam was a different story. Though the refugees, as well as the millions who had no option but to stay, suffered hardship, they were not subject to the brutality that took place in Cambodia. World Vision, however, was unable to continue serving the people in Vietnam, Cambodia or Laos. A third of all our field work was gone. Over fifty of our staff and their families had been evacuated losing all their possessions. An unknown number of staff members who remained lost their lives. So much of what we had attempted in all three countries seemed doomed to futility.

Recalling this dark moment, Vietnam director Don Scott wrote, "This will always stand out for me personally as a time of heartache. The tragedy of this time remains as a vivid reminder of the fruitlessness of war."

It was one of the darkest moments in our history.

PICKING UP THE PIECES

Dietrich Bonhoeffer wrote from prison, "The character of a man is revealed less by his achievements than by his sufferings." The same could be said of organizations.

In 1975 there was little time to brood over the calamity that had engulfed us. Nearly 30,000 sponsors lost touch with their sponsored children and knew nothing of their fate. These people shared our grief and most were willing to transfer their assistance to a child elsewhere. Many kept their monthly support coming to help develop new programs for children.

We turned first to other countries of Asia where World Vision already worked, and then to Latin America. There was no question about the needs of children. The issue was how to respond in a way that could be managed and did not create dependency. Working through existing contacts, childcare director Edmund Janss started programs in Brazil, Colombia, Ecuador, Guatemala and Mexico. Within six months this massive shift in focus had been completed, although problems emerged in later years due to the pressure of rapid expansion. It takes time to build trust in project communities as a basis for partnership. The quality of the work suffered in places where these relationships had not no time to develop.

Meanwhile, a horror of unimaginable proportions unfolded in Cambodia, while the rest of the world looked on, glad to wash its hands of the Vietnam War.

"What did they say in the West about the evacuation of Phnom Penh?" asked a refugee in an interview. He had lost every member of his family.

It had all been reported in the press; the three million inhabitants of Phnom Penh forced at gunpoint to walk out of their homes with only the clothes they wore for the long march into the countryside, hospitals emptied of their patients with those in beds pushed out into the streets, hundreds of thousands crowding the roads out of Phnom Penh, old people collapsing, sick children dying by the roadside, the stragglers beaten to death "to save bullets."

"Tell me," repeated the refugee, "how did the Free World react?"

Perhaps he imagined demonstrations in the streets of Paris and New York, or London or Sydney. The interviewer did not have the heart to tell him that almost no one spoke out.

In an address in 1975 to a big Los Angeles church that had mounted intense opposition to the Vietnam War, I pointed out that, while an estimated two million people died in the Vietnam tragedy amidst the sustained outrage of the entire world, almost that many were coldly, deliberately, mercilessly butchered in Cambodia by the Khmer Rouge, while the world went about its business in deafening silence.

PEOPLE IN SEARCH OF A FUTURE

We kept praying for Vietnam, Cambodia and Laos — praying for their people, praying for a door of opportunity to open once again so that we could return. When Vietnamese refugees in utter desperation put to sea in anything that would float, World Vision urged governments and the United Nations to rescue them from the dangerous, pirate-plagued waters of the South China Sea. No one was interested.

Stan Mooneyham took up the cause of the boat people. Eventually, we purchased a 188-foot, 345-ton ship, registered it in Honduras, refurbished it, named it *Seasweep* and, against all kinds of opposition, mounted a rescue operation.

Seasweep became both a haven for the lost and a message to an indifferent world. The cause was taken up by others. France, Norway, Germany and Italy all sent ships. When there was no longer a need for *Seasweep* on the high seas, the UN High Commissioner for Refugees contracted the ship to bring medical care to boat refugees in island transit camps.

Hundreds of thousands of other refugees made their way through the jungle from Cambodia and Laos to border camps in Thailand. It takes a certain kind of courage to become a refugee. To leave the familiar place, abandon one's home, leave behind all possessions, break ties with loved ones, endure the hardship and dangers of the road or bush and face an uncertain future. I often reminded our field teams to be sensitive to what people had gone through; to be aware of their grief, their sense of loss for the past and their anxiety about the future. These emotional needs must not be overlooked in meeting the immediate needs for food, shelter and medical care.

With the Vietnamese occupation of Cambodia in 1979, our efforts to serve the survivors of Pol Pot's reign of terror were renewed. Since the Hanoi government was not recognized by the United States, approaches were made through World Vision Australia to the Cambodian Ambassador in Hanoi. The Ambassador urged World Vision to respond to the desperate needs in his country, promising entry visas.

When the visas were granted, Stan Mooneyham, with an Australian team including Roger Walker, who had obtained the visas, took a plane load of medical supplies, food and emergency items to Phnom Penh. They were greeted at the deserted airport by a security officer, who walked up to Stan and said in English, "I remember you. You spoke at the stadium. We have been hoping you would return!"

For a long moment Stan was unable to speak. It was a stunning and gracious encouragement from God at the very start of our mission. After some delay, permission to enter Cambodia was granted. The team met with Mr. Hun Sen, then Foreign Minister and later Cambodia's second prime minister. World Vision's Cambodia director, Jaisankar Sarma recalled that visit. "Stan Mooneyham took a penknife," he said, "made a cut in his wrist and explained that though his skin color was white, the color of his blood was the same as the blood of Cambodians." An agreement was reached for World Vision to resume work. We had been given a second chance.

Stan Mooneyham and I, with other colleagues, went to Cambodia two months later to assess the kind of work most needed. We saw a stricken country, grieving for its dead. The task of physical reconstruction was colossal; the human damage could never be repaired.

Phnom Penh was like a ghost city, its streets littered with wreckage. The people were afraid, unwilling to trust anyone. Everyone we met had lost at least one family member, many had seen their whole families die, or had been separated, never to see them again. The Vietnamese, as both liberators and oppressors, controlled everything.

Mere children, 12 or 13 years old, roamed the streets carrying automatic weapons. The future was too far off to think about; survival today was enough.

SEEDS OF HOPE IN THE KILLING FIELDS

I have learned over the years to look for signs of hope like points of light when everything seems dark. And Cambodia in January 1980 was very dark.

Our team traveled 200 miles north to Siem Riep over atrocious roads. Stopping at a village for a brief rest, we noticed a large group of children gathered around an elderly woman. We exchanged greetings and went on our way. Two days later we stopped at the same place on the return trip. There they were again. We decided to investigate.

Mrs. Chap Kem was a widow. Her husband and eight children had all perished under the Khmer Rouge. After the Vietnamese came, she returned to her village to find fifteen children orphaned and alone. Despite her own grief and poverty, she had taken them all in! Her simple but loving care was reflected in the health and happy faces of the children.

We discovered that Chap Kem was a Christian, one of a handful in the village. She showed us her worn New Testament, hidden and preserved through the nightmare.

"Could we sing a hymn?" she asked through our interpreter.

She remembered *What A Friend We Have In Jesus,* taught to her by the missionaries.

Picture a tiny thatched house of one room, raised up about six feet on bamboo stilts and set among tall palm trees. A cooking pot simmered on the smoking embers of a small fire in the open space under the house. Freshly washed clothes were strung out to dry, forcing us to duck our heads as we crowded underneath to shelter from the sun. Here was life at its simplest.

We held hands — Chap Kem, smiling children and tall foreigners speaking a strange language. There we sang, with all the stories of suffering and grief fresh in our minds,

Have we trials and temptations,
          is there trouble anywhere?
We should never be discouraged;
          take it to the Lord in prayer.
Can we find a friend so faithful
          who will all our sorrows share?
Jesus knows our every weakness;
          take it to the Lord in prayer.

No cathedral could have been more grand, no congregation more inspired. Here was hope. Here was courage. Here was all the compassion of God residing in one loving heart. Our job in World Vision is to discover and nurture these seeds of hope, from which new life springs.

Little by little we started the program, concentrating on the rehabilitation of small industries to help produce food; fishing nets and boats, poultry and livestock, farming tools and seed, a condensed milk factory. Rice distribution was undertaken in Takeo Province.

Permission was also obtained to refurbish the hospital we had built five years earlier. It had been ready to begin work the week before the Khmer Rouge took Phnom Penh. They had used it for an army barracks, leaving it dirty but not badly damaged. It has served as the National Pediatric Hospital for the past 15 years.

Stan Mooneyham's "love affair with Cambodia" had come full circle. He later had the joy of seeing the Christian Church officially recognized in 1990 after fifteen years of persecution and denial. He had worked tirelessly for this during and after his presidency of World Vision.

In 1993 the National Pediatric Hospital was dedicated to the memory of Stan Mooneyham. I was asked to provide a quote for the memorial plaque. I chose the words I had first heard from Stan in Cambodia twenty years before:

"Love talked about is easily turned aside; love demonstrated is irresistible."

In World Vision, I am engaged in a continuing journey, a journey that has brought me to places where I had never been before. It has brought me to the rugged roads of the poor and oppressed. It has taken me to the dusty streets of the marginalized and the underprivileged. All I had for these people before were pity and sympathy. I thought that was already good of me. World Vision has taught me to cross over this emotional boundary. I have learned to admire the poor's wisdom and ability to make their own world.

— Joey Umali, World Vision Philippines

5

The Road Is Long

The place is Sydney Airport, in 1970. Stan Mooneyham is arriving from Asia for a speaking tour of Australia and New Zealand. A well-attended press conference begins.

"Dr. Mooneyham, do you work in India?"

"Only in a small way," replies Stan. "India is a country of vast poverty, needing long-term help. Our job is immediate relief."

That was our position in 1970. But we would soon learn to take a fresh look at our traditional welfare approach. We discovered that you cannot be satisfied with welfare if you want to help people transform their own world.

Emergency relief is essential when life is threatened, but it does not equip the poor to change their future. It is like pulling a drowning man from the water, only to watch him fall in again. The move towards development was inevitable as we "peeled the onion" of human need.

THE SCANDAL OF POVERTY

Bangladesh is a good example of the massive poverty that traps two-thirds of the world's population. My first visit to the country took me into an intensely personal encounter with poverty. I was to visit a project among displaced people on the island of Demra in the vast Ganges delta. Before going to the project, Mary Campbell, our New Zealand nurse, wanted to see a 12-year-old boy she had brought to the Dacca Hospital a few days earlier.

"Don't spit scatterdly," said a sign in the lobby of the hospital. The wry humor of the sign did not seem funny any more as the sights, smells and sounds of suffering hit me. We climbed dark stairways, made our way through crowded, stifling wards. When we approached our little patient it was obvious something was very wrong. Some kind of commotion was going on in the center of the ward.

We hurried over to find the boy on a stretcher, with a young Bengali doctor working over him. The doctor's face was strained, dripping beads of perspiration. Several nurses were by his elbow with emergency equipment, other patients watching the drama like an audience at a theater-in-the-round. The father, tortured and wracked by grief, stood to one side. Now I was drawn into the drama too. "Is there no way to help? Can't the doctor do something?" The struggle became my struggle. I wanted so much to fan up that little spark of life.

But everything possible had already been done. The doctor straightened up and slowly shook his head. The nurses removed the intravenous drip. The spark had gone out. Chiand Mia was dead.

Chiand Mia lived for only twelve years. He had no toys, never went to school, never had a bed other than the one he died in. His family had been living on the streets most of his life — father, mother, two sisters and Chiand.

I decided to see for myself where Chiand had lived and suffered. Demra is not the kind of tropical island you see in the travel ads. It is flat, bare, dusty and exposed to the violent winds that sometimes sweep down from the north. It reminded me of the back of some gigantic whale to which 35,000 people clung. They did not choose to live there. As usual, they had no choice. One night they were rounded up at gunpoint from the streets of Dacca and taken to this remote place where they would not be a visible embarrassment to the authorities. There they were dumped, with no housing, no food, no facilities, no water — nothing. They were simply left to die — and hundreds did.

In one of the wretched hovels made of sacking, mud and a few sticks, Chiand had lived with his family. The shelter was perhaps four feet high and about ten feet by six in area. There was no furniture of any kind. There Chiand had become ill. His mother tried her best to make him comfortable, tried to obtain a little extra nourishment to strengthen his frail body. She did not know that he was in the early stages of typhoid fever. After two weeks, when it became clear that Chiand needed help, she took him to the World Vision clinic run by Mary Campbell. But it was too late.

Death is always shattering, especially when it claims the young. The trouble is that in a country like Bangladesh one tends to accept suffering as part of the landscape. In a way, it is easier to cope with the suffering of a whole nation or of a needy world from a distance than to come face-to-face with the suffering of one person, one family. We too casually shrug off the larger suffering as something the people have become used to. In one sense they have. There's a culture of poverty that afflicts the very poor like Chiand Mia and his family.

The culture of poverty offers absolutely no options, no choice at all. No choice about what you will eat, where you will live, what you will wear, where you will go. You are totally locked into the inevitable. You are crushed by overwhelming circumstances that grind you to dust. You accommodate yourself to inconvenience and suffering. When it rains you get wet; when it's muddy you get dirty; when there's no food your stomach aches; when you get sick you die. You can't change it. You can't fight it. You can't help it. In the end you accept it. It's a kind of cultural suicide. Poverty like this is a festering sore on the face of humanity. It is not the way the Creator intended it to be.

Michel Quoist in *Prayers of Life* puts it this way:

I am not made of plaster, God says, nor of stone, nor of bronze.

I am living flesh, throbbing, suffering.

I am among men, and they have not recognized me.

I am poorly paid, I am unemployed, I live in a slum, I have tuberculosis,

I sleep under bridges, I am patronized.

And yet I said to them, "Whatever you do to them, however humble, you do to me."

That's clear.

The worst is that they know it, but that they don't take it seriously.

They have broken my heart, God says.

Welfare or emergency relief cannot release people from this kind of poverty. You cannot just change things, least of all by providing money. A completely different approach is needed, which we call "transformational development."

AGENTS OF CHANGE

Gene Daniels, our director in Indonesia in the late 1960s and early 1970s, was the first World Vision person I heard speak of community development. At a conference in 1971 he described a project for raising ducks. Raising ducks! "What has that got to do with World Vision?" was the implied, but unasked question. Everyone heard Gene out politely.

He went back to Indonesia and quietly experimented. Gene introduced a program called Pioneers for Community Development. The idea was to recruit young Indonesians in specialized areas such as agriculture or health. They would be people who were prepared to devote two or three years of their lives to live in an impoverished community, gain the trust of the local people and gradually help them accept, understand and practice improved ways of doing things. These were Christian young people, able to bring the kind of dedication needed, equipped by experience and training to share their faith in Jesus Christ, who is the true agent of transformation.

Five years later I saw the result of this approach in the steamy jungle of Kalimantan, formerly Borneo. We were to visit the village of Lerak, inland from Sinkawang on Kalimantan's west coast. To reach Lerak you fly to Pontianak on the Equator, drive 150 miles to Sinkawang, another 60 miles by road to Sambas and finally 30 miles by canoe. The last part of our canoe trip took us through thick, overhanging jungle. Many times we had to get out and lift the canoe over fallen logs.

Eventually we reached Lerak, where laughing children waited on the bank to welcome us. These were Dyak people and I remembered seeing pictures of the children before the project started. The swollen bellies, discolored hair, and festering sores of malnutrition had disappeared. The transformation had to be seen to be believed.

As we got out of the canoe, an old man met us. He was eager to offer us refreshments, so we climbed a wobbly ladder to his tiny house on stilts above the ground. He seated us on small stools and served papaya, pineapple and bananas. He had been the village witch doctor and was the last person to become a Christian. Everyone else had become believers in Jesus Christ. The whole village! He showed us a little earthenware bowl with a tiny heap of ashes in it where he had burned his idols and fetishes, symbols to him of old superstitions.

I learned that, having become Christians, the village leaders were seeking reconciliation with the neighboring village. They had once been a single community, but separated when fighting erupted ten years before. Now a little church had been built between the two villages as a symbol of reconciliation.

The introduction of the Christian gospel is often criticized by development specialists as cultural interference. But our experience shows us that when the gospel is not forced, but shared with sensitivity and respect for the dignity of people, the development process is enhanced, not undermined. I saw a whole community transformed. Where once there was despair, now there was hope. Where darkness, now light. Where death, now life.

We walked along a jungle path and saw rubber trees being tapped. The raw latex was dried and pressed in a giant wringer ready for market. We took off our shoes and waded through the mud to a rice paddy. Above us on the mountainside a great swath of cleared forest was evidence of the old slash and burn method of agriculture — destructive, wasteful and unproductive. However, the rice paddy had become overgrown after the first season and the people had to be encouraged to persevere. Change is hard work.

Individual houses, with their own safe water storage from the abundant rain, had replaced the old longhouses of the Dyaks. Vegetable gardens had been cultivated around the houses. Mothers had been taught how to prepare the vegetables, cereals and fish. Literacy classes had begun for men and women.

"Where are the toilets?" asked Gene Daniels. There was an awkward silence — the people were still using the river. The plan to build latrines had been put aside. Still more work to be done, and the reason for it needed to be explained again.

How had all this happened? What brought about the change? I met three young men: a teacher, an agriculturalist and an evangelist. Their professional training had been sponsored by World Vision and now they were supported as "pioneers for community development." What we saw was the result of three years of patient effort, not by foreigners, but by young Indonesians.

The same afternoon we walked several miles to the neighboring village. Here there were no growing crops, no neat new houses, no smiling faces. The people lived in the traditional longhouses with their slat floors, through which rubbish was dropped for the dogs and pigs underneath. I watched a mother stuff rice balls into her baby's throat, almost choking the child. A dog ate from the same bowl.

But the possibility of change was not far off. The people of Lerak were sharing their new life with their former enemies.

That was one of the best signs that transformational development was happening.

As we worshiped in the church that night, led by a pastor on his monthly visit, the rain began to fall. And how it fell! I lay awake in my bunk in the small team house that night listening to the deluge and wondering how we would get out, until sleep overtook me.

I awoke to a clear sky. But a raging torrent roared by the village in place of yesterday's stream. The creek had risen six feet in the night. The whole village gathered to see us off. They were used to this and thought it a great joke. To me, white-water canoeing was a new adventure, and no joke. Sent on our way by their "God be with you," we waved goodbye and started our hair-raising journey. We shot over great logs that yesterday we had climbed under. But we made it!

Back in Jakarta I thought of those young people now far away, buried in a remote jungle village. Agents of change, not imposing new ways, but walking alongside the people in a journey of discovery. One of them, James Tumbuan, once a sponsored child in World Vision's childcare program, was destined to become the executive director of World Vision Indonesia in years to come.

In 1974, "development for self reliance" became part of our revised basic objectives. Gene and others had made their point. Under the leadership of former U.S. Army Colonel, Hal Barber, World Vision's long walk down the development road began officially.

MAKING A CRITICAL DIFFERENCE

Development starts, not with grand plans, but with simple steps that build confidence and trust. It starts with people where they are, with what they know. Take the case of Heenepella, a village community in Shri Lanka. I had gone there to see the effect of a revolving-loan program World Vision had introduced. But the process did not start as a revolving loan fund. It went back much further.

Heenepella was a depressed community so poor that its people were totally rejected by the rest of society. Food prepared by them would not be touched, no one would perform weddings or funerals for them, no one would buy products made by them. They were social and economic outcasts.

When contact was first made by World Vision Lanka staff, the people were suspicious. Any sort of communication was difficult. However, our project officer, Dudley Wijesinghe, did learn that the care of children during the day was a problem. Survival depended on both parents working in the fields. No one was left to mind the children. By helping the community discuss the problem together and agree to cooperate, our team enabled them to devise a simple system of rotation to mind the children. As trust grew, we planted some vegetable gardens and arranged for a nutritionist to demonstrate how children's health could be improved with a better diet.

Basic sanitation was next. All the children had worms and other intestinal problems. Impure water and the lack of toilets was the cause. Dudley explained why it was essential to install proper latrines, to wash hands and to boil drinking water. This took time and patience. But the people were interested now. They had already seen that change was possible and that by working together their lives could be different. Dudley told the people that concrete pit covers for deep-pit latrines were available free from the local government. World Vision would provide materials for walls and roof, if the community would do the work. My visit coincided with the official opening of the completed toilets. I went from toilet to toilet, cutting ribbons and inspecting the construction. The people were justifiably proud of what they had accomplished.

But that was not all. The relationship built up by the World Vision team had enabled the people to share their greatest burden. In earlier bad times they had been forced to borrow money to survive, offering their land as security. A portion of every crop was demanded in payment, sometimes up to 50 percent of the yield. They were slaves on their own land, unable to repay the wealthy moneylenders.

In cooperation with the Rural Development Society, a local infrastructure throughout Shri Lanka, World Vision established a revolving loan fund sufficient to pay off all the loans, about U.S. $1,500 total. The Rural Development Society would pay the moneylenders, then create new loans at 5 percent interest to be repaid by each family. This they could manage. The day of my visit was "pay day." The district member of parliament had been invited to ensure that justice was done, since it was against the law for any lender to refuse repayment.

What a day this was! Everyone was there — the women in their best saris, the men aglow with new confidence, the children now healthier and stronger. The "official party" stood at a table in the center of a clearing, with all the people gathered before us. As the names were called, I handed out each repayment in cash on behalf of the Society, receiving the cancelled loan agreement in return.

When the last loan was paid, the member of parliament made a rousing speech urging the people to take responsibility for their future. The whole village then erupted into celebration: clapping, cheering, dancing. It was a moment of profound liberation, something they had never dreamed possible. The politician then led the way to a table spread with food prepared by the villagers in a remarkable reversal of the previous rejection. Several weeks later a mass wedding was conducted, legalizing the family relationships. The new loans were later set up, and a formal evaluation seven years later showed a 90 percent repayment record for the new loans.

The Heenepella story began with small, simple steps. But they made the critical difference, providing a starting point. Each step forward (and some backward) gave confidence and insight that enabled another step to be taken.

STARTING OUT ON A LONG ROAD

In the West African country of Burkina Faso, I once went to a village at the fringe of the Sahara Desert where we had helped the community drill wells, establish gardens and improve their animals. The drive out in our two vehicles was long, hot and dusty. The road was merely a track in places and difficult to see. When we arrived we were greeted by a festive celebration. The whole village toured the project with us before we came back for singing, prayers, dancing, speeches and, of course, a feast.

I can close my eyes now and see the scene as if it were yesterday. Darkness had fallen, the dense darkness of a remote desert village. Our faces were lit by the flames of torches made from large sticks, bound at one end with grass dipped in fat. We had little idea of what we were eating, which may have been just as well! When all the talking ended, a quiet hush fell on us all. We prayed. Then one of our companions said to the village chief in the local dialect, "The road is long. We ask for the road." It was the traditional way of asking permission to leave.

"I give you the road," the chief replied.

The road was indeed long and very difficult in the dark. We strayed occasionally from the route, we had two tire punctures and a breakdown. But at last we arrived safely home.

Transformational development is like that long road. It is neither simple nor easy. It takes time. It takes patience. There is much to learn, especially from the poor themselves. There are failures and disappointments. Large numbers of people, especially in crowded cities, are so desperately marginalized and disoriented from any kind of decent existence that there seems no way out.

Not every story ends like Lerak or Heenepella, and even those that do later see reversals. But that's what it means to trust people. They have to own the development process, just as every human being is ultimately responsible for his or her own life. Those who wish to help may walk alongside, but not take over. Development is not something you "do" for people.

You can only help create the conditions, give encouragement and carefully offer some resources that do not replace, but add to, what the people already have within themselves and around them.

The organization that undertakes development had better be prepared for change within itself. To start with, there are usually contradictions in style and attitude that have to change. Charles Elliott puts it well in his book, *Comfortable Compassion?*

Poor people in poor countries do not naturally think in terms of projects. They do not think in the bureaucratically convenient categories of aid agencies and government finance officers. The truer one seeks to be to their perspectives, their priorities, their understanding of their own situation, the more difficult it becomes to design the kind of neat, hard-edged, time-bound project so beloved by the development industry.

The aggressive, "can-do" attitude of the West needs to give way to the empowerment principle that allows others to move at their own pace. Sophisticated, well-equipped managers and technicians must exercise restraint, and do so without being patronizing. Cooperation rather than competition may be a new discipline for many.

Secondly, development means longer-term commitments. You cannot "dump and run." You have got to be willing, and able, to sustain a relationship with a community for five, ten or perhaps fifteen years, depending on the size and complexity of the activities that emerge from the relationship. This long-term commitment requires more careful and subtle management of resources than relief programs, for example.

Third, a big organization like World Vision has all kinds of baggage that gets in the way of development: bureaucracy, systems, reports, layers of authority, policies of all kinds and committees. Such an organization is more likely to hinder than to support the process of development.

Fourth, there is the question of control. Traditionally we are used to the donor, or at least, the donor agency, being in control. Some refer to it cynically as "the golden rule" — he who has the gold makes the rules. Development cannot work that way. It can only be effective when the poor themselves are in charge, when they become "owners" of the process and the results. What you are doing in transformational development is according people the dignity of voice and self-determination.

SETTING A NEW COURSE

What about the donor? What do those who give money think about all this? At first it may seem too complicated. But when we see how change happens in our own lives, we recognize the same process. It takes time. It involves personal responsibility. Being part of change for other people opens us up to transformation within ourselves.

These kinds of factors can set up fundamental contradictions within an organization. We have struggled with these tensions in World Vision for a long time, and still do.

We are far from having solved them. We have described ourselves as a "transform" rather than a "transfer" organization. There is a broad consensus about that, but we are still working out what it really means for the organization itself.

Back in the 1970s our formal commitment to development was a major course-change for World Vision. It was a paradigm shift, a fundamental adjustment in the way we thought about ourselves and our world. Not only where we worked, but how we worked became an important issue.

There were even wider implications — how we work together. As the number of countries where we worked increased and adopted the participative style that grows out of a developmental philosophy, the desire for participation and voice in the affairs of the organization also increased. It was the same need we had felt earlier in the Australian office. Traditional categories of "giving" and "receiving" countries started to disappear. The organization began to open up to a process of transformation from within that was only seen in faint outlines then, but would have a profound influence in years to come. As Tom Getman of World Vision's Washington, D.C. office said, "It might well be that God has called us all to the pilgrimage of World Vision as much for our own salvation as for that of those to whom we go."

This spirit was in harmony with a movement that had already begun toward global partnership.

Part III

From Third World To One World

I believe the vision of internationalizing World Vision which Stan Mooneyham, Graeme Irvine and others had in the Seventies was inspired by the Holy Spirit then and the commitment shown by the Partnership today to follow it through is rooted in our acceptance of that idea and our desire to make it into a reality.

— Don Scott, World Vision Canada

6

A Vision Of Partnership

W hen it grows in size and scope, an organization reaches certain stages that require a quantum shift in philosophy, relationships or structure. By 1970 World Vision had reached that stage.

Canada and Australia, as newer donor countries (or support countries, as we called them), felt the need for a say in how and where funds were spent. They also wanted to share in discussions on policy, strategic decisions and long-term direction. This was not so much a desire for control as it was a need for accountability to donors and a sense of participation. The field countries also felt a need at least to be heard, if not to be represented, at the decision-making table.

Stan Mooneyham, who was taking over as the new president at that time, perceived this mood. It did not take him by surprise and was not the result of pressure. It was already part of his own world-view. I was present at a conference of World Vision's country directors in 1971, when he described four eras in the modern missionary movement.

First, a *pioneering* era, which generally accompanied colonial expansion from Europe.

Then came an *institutional* phase as the missions started schools, hospitals, seminaries, farms, hostels, printing presses and welfare services of all kinds. Following World War II a powerful swing to *nationalism* emerged as colonial empires crumbled.

The new frontier, Stan said, was *internationalism,* calling Christians to true partnership across national and cultural boundaries.

BEYOND PATERNALISM

Two months later Stan Mooneyham brought together a representative group to think through some of these ideas. He called it the *International Council.* It had no authority to act, but would advise the president and the board. Nine board and executive leaders from the United States, Canada and Australia were there; also Bishop Chandu Ray of Pakistan and Dr. Han Kyung Chik of Korea.

We had a sense of breaking new ground for World Vision. Everyone contributed to the lively discussion. Dr. Han, who was a central figure in the early years with Bob Pierce, stressed the importance of national boards in all countries where World Vision worked. Bishop Ray warned about the artificial and corrupting power of money. These statements from Dr. Han and Bishop Ray illustrated the importance of hearing voices that challenged fairly-typical Western assumptions and opened doors to change.

In summing up our two days together, the president committed World Vision to:

a) steadfastly resist all feelings of cultural and racial imperialism,

b) earnestly seek to develop true love and high regard for God's people everywhere, and

c) accept with gratitude and humility the place God gives us to serve.

From this meeting a small committee chaired by Dr. Carlton Booth was formed to look at the structures of other international organizations. Carlton Booth had been a member of World Vision's Board of Directors almost from the beginning. He had worked closely with Bob Pierce and knew our history intimately. Dr. Booth's committee studied 14 organizations. While some interesting ideas came out of the study, no structure seemed to fit World Vision.

Two years later a larger group met in Thailand to receive Carlton Booth's report and explore further our international structure. Stan Mooneyham had decided the original International Council was not sufficiently representative and replaced it in Thailand with what he called the "joint boards"; that is, the boards of World Vision in the United States, Canada and Australia. Several Asian church leaders were again invited.

Our vision for a new kind of international framework started to take hold. We agreed to form a special Internationalization Study Committee to recommend a basis for "a true partnership among all national entities; a partnership of both structure and spirit."

All this sounds very formal. But, as with the 1972 meeting, we felt we were at the edge of something exciting and historic. Stan asked me to chair the new study committee, which comprised both board and staff members. We were to report to a further meeting of joint boards in two years. There was no time to lose. Remember that the

Indochina crisis took place during this period, as well as my move to the United States.

Over the next two years we put our hearts and minds to the challenge. The process of internationalization, as we called it, was never seen as an end in itself. Our chief concern was not to be politically correct, but to fulfill our mission more effectively.

The joint boards, now including New Zealand, met again in Honolulu in April 1976 to receive the Internationalization Study Committee's report. In presenting the report I stated:

We recognize that the ultimate goal of internationalization is not structure but function. The ministry must be better performed, and people in need must be more effectively cared for.

We defined "internationalization" as a process of growth in partnership. The emphasis was not on creating an international partnership between our several national offices. That already existed. Our aim was to make it more effective.

At the core we saw partnership not as structure, or even as process, but an attitude toward each other — an attitude that did not see one partner as superior to any other. We wanted a mutual acceptance and accountability to each other based on the spiritual connection that held us together as members of the Body of Christ. What we were looking for were ways of expressing that connection in tangible, organizational terms.

Finally, I talked about the element of risk:

There is a sense in which we must learn as we go along. If we step too far, too quickly, we step badly. And not to step at all is to shrink from the risk of faith. It requires little faith to take a step that involves little risk. Lord Wavell, Viceroy of India during the critical years prior to the transfer of power from Britain, wrote in his diary, referring to the India Committee of the British cabinet, "They profess their desire to give India self-government, but they will take no risk to make it possible."

Over a period of four days we heard each other, expressed our hopes and fears and considered various alternatives. We did not want a majority vote, but a consensus of mind and spirit so that we could go forward in unity.

By the end of the week we were of one mind and decided unanimously to form World Vision International as an organizational entity distinct from any of the present national structures. The existing donor countries (United States, Canada, Australia and New Zealand) became members of the new corporation. Steps were put in motion to develop the legal and administrative framework for the new World Vision International over the ensuing two years.

In 1978 we met again to adopt a *Declaration of Internationalization* and formally constitute World Vision International. We had embarked on another stage of our venture in partnership.

OUR GRAND EXPERIMENT

Had we agreed on a fabulous formula that solved all our problems? No! We had merely taken the first step. Some saw it as a radical and even dangerous step. Might we not lose control, undermine the unique character of World Vision as envisaged by the founder? Others saw the move as a fairly modest start toward something ultimately more mature. One thing was clear — internationalization was not merely an event that happened in 1978. The process had been under way before then and was still going on.

At first the donor countries played the dominant role, but right from the beginning we had a vision of partnership that we believed would ultimately include as full partners all countries where World Vision worked. Even as early as the Honolulu meeting, an Australian board member, John Denton, urged that recipient nations be fully part of the partnership. He recognized that our initial structure was international only in Western terms. Over the years greater balance has evolved, and continues to evolve.

The question of control was bound to arise. Who "calls the shots?" One board member once said to me bluntly, "The provider should control." That is not the spirit of partnership. Nor do I believe it is the spirit of Jesus Christ. The gospels are full of examples of trust rather than control, trust that is based on commitments and relationships.

One of the best-known stories in the Bible, the parable of the Good Samaritan, which is often associated with the work of World Vision, contains this same dimension of trust. "Look after him," said the Samaritan to the innkeeper, "and when I come again I will repay you" (Luke 10:35). The whole question of "giving and receiving" had long been debated in World Vision and we are starting to grasp the idea of "mutual stewardship of ministry," wherever a country might be on the spectrum of giving or receiving funds.

That was the vision of partnership held by those who set us on the course. We also understand more fully that giving and receiving involves more than money. There is an exchange of values, faith and life that goes beyond the transfer of funds.

We have called internationalization "our grand experiment." To some it made no sense. It was not the way big corporations did business. But then, they were not engaged in the process of human transformation as we were. The business you are in affects the way you organize yourself to do it.

Some saw World Vision as a highly complex organization. In some ways it is, especially if you think in terms of traditional management structures. But in essence it is simple — just as simple as the structure (if you could call it that) put in place by Jesus for the greatest enterprise on earth. "I give you a new commandment," he said. "Love one another" (John 13:34).

The great Scottish preacher and scientist, Henry Drummond, writing 100 years ago, described Jesus' method of sending out a small group of men and women unheralded to revolutionize the world:

They went about, did good, sowed seed, died and and lived again in the lives of those they helped. These in turn, a fraction of them, did the same. They met, they prayed, they talked of Christ, they loved, they went among others, and by act and word passed on their secret.

War might have won for Christ's cause a passing victory; wealth might have purchased a superficial triumph; political power might have gained a temporary success. But in these there is no note of universality, of solidarity, of immortality. To live through the centuries and pervade the uttermost ends of the earth, to stand while kingdoms tottered and civilizations changed, to survive fallen churches and crumbling creeds — there was no soil for the Kingdom of God like the hearts of common men and women. Some who have written about this Kingdom have emphasized its moral grandeur, others its universality, others its adaptation. I confess what strikes me most is the miracle of its simplicity.[1]

The simplicity of World Vision lies not in its structures, which will always need to change to meet changing conditions, but in its basis of trust and relationship, its ideal of mutual accountability, common stewardship of ministry and equal dignity of all before God. It will be undermined when some try to hold control or take control, to carry on political maneuvers, or seek to gain competitive advantage over a sister, a brother or another group or office.

We need always to remember, too, where ultimate success lies. It is not in how fast things are done (although we need to know when and how to move quickly when human life is at stake), or how much money is raised (although we must never squander the opportunities God gives), or who gets the credit (although recognition of another is honest and right), or how well our global partnership works (although our ability to work globally in unity directly affects the mission).

Success lies in the fulfillment of the mission God has given. That is our priority — not favorite parts of it, but all of it.

A NEW DIRECTION FOR THE FUTURE

In summary, the decision taken in Honolulu in 1976 to create an international partnership with all members accountable to each other, and this on the basis of covenant relationships, set a new direction that would have profound implications for the future.

1. Sermon by Henry Drummond.

The decision represented a truly great step of faith and vision on the part of the board and leadership of World Vision in the the United States. The U.S. was the founding country and by far the largest contributor — two thirds of all World Vision's resources at the time. Yet its leaders were willing to relinquish control and be part of a larger fellowship, in which their views would be respected, but not necessarily prevail. (There may have been times subsequently when some of our U.S. colleagues had second thoughts!)

I believe it is also significant that it was an American, Stan Mooneyham, who had the vision for internationalization and saw it through to implementation. In my opinion, it was Stan's most strategic contribution to World Vision — one of the best things we could have done despite the pressures of the worst times.

In our World Vision terminology we have come to refer to the whole organization worldwide as the World Vision Partnership, meaning all the member countries, with World Vision International being the legally registered coordinating body.

There is no question in my mind that, despite the challenges and frustrations we often experience in our partnership structure (and I have experienced them at least as much and over a longer period than most others), we are a more effective organization because of it, given the nature of our mission. We have a remarkable opportunity in our own organization to discover and demonstrate the principles of global relationship that I believe will be needed in the world of the 21st century.

The Partnership Grows

The process of internationalization between 1975 and 1978 coincided with World Vision's entry to Africa, Latin America, Europe (East and West) and the Middle East. However, it was never our aim to plant a World Vision flag in every country of the world, to pursue a policy of expansion for its own sake. We were not interested in a World Vision empire. Each initiative to begin work in a country arose from special circumstances, or an invitation from interested groups, churches or individuals.

For example, we first went to Africa because of critical food shortages. Once World Vision became known on the continent, especially through church networks, requests came from many countries for assistance. Wherever possible we continued to work through existing channels, preferably inter-church associations for relief and development.

Frequently an emergency relief response to a natural disaster would open the door. That is how we began in Latin America, when Nicaragua was hit by a massive earthquake. Later the loss of our childcare programs in Indochina led us to extend to other countries of Latin America.

Some people within World Vision questioned whether we were spread too thinly. Better to concentrate on fewer countries for greater impact and more strategic use of resources, they said.

I understood the logic of this position. A systematic approach to assessing the need for World Vision in any country was important, taking into account the many factors that determined if and how we should get involved. Part of the assessment involved consulting with people in the country, including other agencies that already worked there. We had developed processes for this kind of analysis.

As an organization we needed to be willing to leave a country or a project if we considered our work completed; also, if conditions did not allow us to operate with integrity. We had made that hard decision at times. On the other hand, it was not always possible to foresee the outcomes of ministry. In many areas we had taken a first step on the basis of the best knowledge available, believing that insights as to the next move would emerge from having taken that step. My own view was that this was a fundamental principle of the development process as well as the life of faith.

Yet each of these positions had validity under certain circumstances. We needed to maintain flexibility and be open to the unusual and different rather than become locked into rigid procedures. This intent to be flexible was part of World Vision's ethos. If I would have reviewed and evaluated the past twenty-five years, I doubt that I would have said we should or should not have gone to this or that country. In many cases we could and should have handled our entry to a country better. I did believe, nevertheless, that each opportunity, in its own way, positioned World Vision for a strategic contribution to the work of Christ.

PENETRATING THE IRON CURTAIN

The Eastern Europe ministry illustrates my point. We knew from our contacts that the churches behind the Iron Curtain were making valiant efforts to maintain their ministry and serve people in need. Their need was for encouragement and sensitive support. Could we help?

We found the person we needed right at our front door. Ralph Hamburger was associate pastor at the church where the Mooneyham family worshiped. His fairly heavy accent indicated he had originally come from Europe, but that was only the tip of the proverbial iceberg.

Ralph was born in Hamburg, Germany and later taken by his family to Holland before World War II. There he experienced the trauma of the Nazi invasion. During the occupation Ralph served with the Dutch Resistance Movement. He does not talk about it much, but one senses the deep emotional scars of those terrible years.

After the war, Ralph migrated to the United States and later prepared for the Christian ministry at Princeton Theological College. Quiet-spoken, generous of heart, possessed of great inner strength and integrity, Ralph is a man that one instinctively trusts. God had prepared him uniquely for Eastern Europe.

These were oppressed countries, each with its distinctive character and needs. Ralph worked quietly in a sensitive service of friendship, counseling and encourage-ment. He spoke four languages and knew the territory. Moving out from his home office in Bonn he built a network of pastors and Christian workers, men and women of great courage who maintained hope in the midst of despair. They trusted him and loved him.

Small items of equipment were provided to support their work — a typewriter here, a duplicating machine there, a bicycle somewhere else. Occasionally Ralph would recommend a larger response such as the provision of a small car or support for a major project. He would often carry with him small gifts of coffee, chocolate and other food items for families suffering discrimination. Despite all their discouragements, the people in Ralph's network had a vision for the future.

Fran and I were once with Ralph in East Berlin. The whole atmosphere was depressing: the weather was bitterly cold, the streets gray and bleak, the people suspicious. Ralph had arranged for us to meet the presiding bishop of the Lutheran Church and his wife. Over afternoon tea in front of their small fire they shared their story. Christians were denied jobs because of their faith. Young people from the church were refused entry to the university. Pressure was put on Christians in countless ways.

"Have you ever considered leaving?" I asked.

"No!" replied the bishop emphatically. "We must keep the church alive for future generations. The day will come when all this will change. We will work and pray for that day."

The day came sooner than expected. History has shown repeatedly that the human spirit will not forever be crushed.

When the Berlin Wall came down and the Iron Curtain finally parted, Ralph Hamburger's patient work of many years had laid the foundation for an enlarged ministry throughout Eastern Europe.

Already we had established a major food distribution program in Poland, working through the Polish Ecumenical Council. World Vision was one of the first organizations to discover and respond to the tragedy of Romania's unwanted children, shut away in wretched orphanages. Dr. Sam Kamaleson, vice president-at-large, conducted renewal conferences for pastors, priests and Christian workers in practically every country of Eastern Europe, including the former Soviet Union.

LATIN AMERICA: A LEARNING LABORATORY

The Latin America childcare program was started to help replace work lost in Indochina. However, the challenge of the continent soon became evident. A comprehensive study was undertaken, including wide consultation throughout the region, to determine priorities and strategy.

In the years that followed, World Vision in Latin America developed its distinctive style and approach. I had a glimpse of this during a visit to the city of Medellin, Colombia.

Ringed by the Andes mountains, Medellin is a big provincial city of nearly 1.5 million people. Apart from its notorious link with the international drug trade, the city has sprawling areas of great poverty. Many of the poor inhabit squatter settlements clinging to the steep slopes of the mountains. It was here that World Vision had begun a ministry three years before my visit. This was an example of the systematic approach. Medellin was clearly a place of enormous need and a process of social analysis led to the decision to develop a program there as part of the country strategy for Colombia.

The approach adopted in Medellin was to conduct a seminar for local clergy. During the three-day seminar, the results of the analysis were shared and World Vision's holistic view of development explained. The pastors had many questions.

Some pastors were excited by what they heard, others were uncertain, some were negative. At the end of the seminar, the pastors were invited to work together on a district basis, facilitated by World Vision, to reach out to the poor. About half wanted to be involved. The World Vision area team in Medellin then worked with the churches and the communities to identify needs and organize themselves in response.

My visit was planned at the same time as a review of progress by the pastors. Again they met and shared their experiences. I later visited several of the projects and discussed progress with the area team. One interesting result was the following statement on *What is a Project?* developed by the World Vision area team:

A project is:
- where learning takes place and experience is gained
- where love is demonstrated
- where the objectives of World Vision become reality
- where donors' expectations are fulfilled
- where the poor meet God
- where the hardest and most important work is done
- where the talking stops and the action starts
- where the face of World Vision is seen
- where the church touches the world
- where numbers become names and plans become people
- where the nerve endings of World Vision are exposed
- where people's gifts are discovered and released
- where transformation begins
- where hope is born

Latin America has become World Vision's foremost laboratory in transformational development through a continuing education process under the leadership of Latin America vice president Manfred Grellert.

CROSSROADS OF THE WORLD

As in Latin America, World Vision went to the Middle East to work with children after the collapse of the ministry in Indo-China. By 1980 we needed to review this work and decide whether to remain involved in the region and, if so, on what basis. I asked a veteran of many years' work in the Middle East, Leonard Rogers, to conduct a study. On the basis of his extensive report we decided to expand the Middle East program, with the focus on Lebanon, Egypt, and the Occupied Territories of West Bank/Gaza. Though we did not expect to build a huge program, we believed we needed to be there.

Standing at the crossroads of three great continents, the Middle Eastern countries from earliest times have been a focal point of trade, religious and cultural encounter, as well as bitter conflict. These ancient lands seem to embody in their history the whole human drama.

The twentieth century is no exception. The weapons are more destructive, the scope of conflict wider and the consequences more far-reaching. Solutions are consequently more complex. The Middle East may indeed be the litmus test of man's capacity to live on this planet in harmony. Just as its bitter hostilities emit waves of tension globally, so the Middle East has the capacity to radiate peace by demonstrating tolerance in diversity.

AN EVER-WIDENING STREAM

The immediate and most visible effect of World Vision's presence in so many countries is the possibility of being a catalyst for change. Often our presence opens up contacts and opportunities for relatively low cost activities that have far-reaching value in the long run.

There's another aspect to it. To attend a World Vision Directors' Conference, which brings together our executive leaders from each country, or an International Council, where board and staff representatives from all World Vision countries meet every three years, is to see an amazing spectrum of nationalities and cultures. The whole planet seems to be represented, creating a richness of thought and perspective which I believe helps us to understand and address issues from a global perspective. It helps position World Vision as an even more effective global player in the challenges that will continue to face humanity.

I once saw a television program that provides a kind of parable for what I am getting at. Titled *The Flight of the Condor,* the program took the viewer on a magnificent sweep of the Andes Cordillera. The picture is a high mountain plateau just before sunrise. It is a frozen world, still, silent, remote. The sun rises in a clear blue sky, casting its first rays over the white wilderness. The camera comes in close on an icicle hanging from a twig. The warming sun melts a drop of water. It falls and is joined by another drop, and then another. Soon a trickle is formed. It in turn joins a little gurgling stream. As a multitude of these tiny tributaries come together, a torrent begins to cascade down the mountainside. It swells and surges, falling hundreds of feet in a splendid waterfall. Reaching the valley floor, it has now become a strong river flowing through dense tropical forest. Other large tributaries flow in to form the mighty Amazon, the world's greatest river. After 3,900 miles it pours into the Atlantic Ocean so powerfully that its current is felt many miles out to sea.

I see in this picture an analogy for the Kingdom of God. The people of Christ representing every culture contribute their gifts to the work of Christ where they are. Most cannot see the whole, or the end result. But they serve faithfully. The Holy Spirit takes all these gifts, merges them into a whole and pours them forth into the great ocean of humanity, where they enrich all of life.

World Vision is part of that picture, a microcosm of the Kingdom if you like. Its incredible diversity enables it to be present in a great variety of contexts — adapting, serving, never exactly the same from place to place — yet held together as one body sharing a common mission of service.

The End Of An Era

Our grand experiment in internationalization had not long been under way when Stan Mooneyham offered his resignation to the Board. Thirteen years of constant travel and exposure to suffering had taken their toll on Stan's health and energy. There were difficulties in his marriage and tensions within World Vision.

It is hard to write about these problems. They are painful for all concerned, and yet to ignore them when you have been close to the events and people is somehow dishonest, or at best leaves too many unanswered questions.

Several of us who had worked alongside Stan encouraged him to step down. He was tired and distracted. He had given strategic leadership to the organization at a critical period in its history and could receive the tributes rightly due to him. There comes a right time in any organization for a new phase of leadership. This seemed the right time for World Vision as well as for Stan.

Sadly, Stan saw this counsel as disloyalty. He left in September 1982 feeling that he no longer had the support from Board and colleagues needed for effective leadership.

Ted Engstrom once again bridged the gap until the appointment of Scotsman Tom Houston. Tom arrived in January 1984 just as the tidal wave of the Ethiopia disaster was about to hit.

It is when the night is darkest that the stars shine the brightest.

— James Mageria, World Vision Africa

7

African Calvary

Just as the 1970s had belonged to Asia with the focus on Vietnam and Cambodia, so in the 1980s the World Vision pendulum swung to Africa. Drought was no stranger to Africa. Food was scarce in many parts of the continent in the mid-'70s. Conflict had also taken its toll of human life in Biafra, Uganda, Angola, Mozambique and elsewhere. But during 1983 there were ominous signs that a catastrophe was approaching beyond anything seen so far. I asked our former international relief director, Tony Atkins, to conduct a survey and to recommend where and how World Vision should respond. Tony traveled extensively through the region and came back with an alarming report that confirmed our worst fears. Ethiopia faced a calamity of unimaginable proportions. Mozambique and Angola were not far behind. Sub-Saharan West Africa faced serious problems, though less severe than the others. Estimates of probable deaths during the next few months ran in the hundreds of thousands.

Tom Houston arrived as we were preparing for action on a bigger scale than anything we had done before. As vice president for field ministries I had proposed a specially augmented field organization to handle the emergency. Relief operations were part of my group; my team had the experience and had acted swiftly to assess and prepare for the crisis.

However, Tom decided to set up a group called the Africa Drought Project to be run separately from the existing field organization. He also chose to lead the Africa Drought Project himself.

I understood the reasons for this project management-type approach, which makes sense for certain kinds of major enterprise. Stan Mooneyham had done the same in the *Seasweep* drama to rescue boat refugees. In fact, Tom chose the executive director of the *Seasweep* operation, Burt Singleton, to assist him with the Africa Drought Project.

The Africa emergency response, however, was very different from *Seasweep*. It was to operate, not on the high seas, but in countries where World Vision was already established, with sensitive networks of relationships in place and future ministry to consider. But the decision was made and the Africa Drought Project went ahead.

World Vision was well-positioned to respond to the emergency in Ethiopia. We knew from our survey where the worst areas were. I had personally visited Ethiopia and had prepared the staff for what seemed like outside intervention. This was often a difficult proposition. The national staff team often felt they had things under control, and usually they did. But there came times when additional resources of people and supply were needed. That was when the solidarity of international partnership came into play.

We had purchased two aircraft and had them in position with trained crews to get personnel and supplies to inaccessible pockets of starvation. In fact, it was our aircraft that carried a film crew to the places where the dreadful images of starvation were first filmed for British television, sending shock waves around the whole world.

MEDIA IGNORES DISASTER

As early as April 1983, World Vision's African journalist, Jacob Akol, wrote widely-distributed articles on the approaching horror. Though published in full in Kenya, the world media decided the aid agencies were "crying wolf."

Akol kept talking to Nairobi-based journalists who filed regular reports to their editors. But Africa was not their priority.

June 1984 found Akol once again in Ethiopia with a World Vision survey team led by Africa relief director Russ Kerr. Masses of people begged for food. By then large numbers were starving. Aid agencies, including World Vision, were stretched to the limit. Akol came back with home video footage of the tragedy and wrote yet another article. "It was my final cry," he said.

He showed the video to Nairobi journalists who were prevented from getting to the scene by the Mengistu government, which were covering up the famine. Eventually, with Akol's help, the BBC team got to the crisis areas on World Vision's aircraft in October 1984, and the rest is history.

When Akol saw the reports on Kenya television he was angry and numb. An outraged world wondered why such a tragedy had been allowed to happen. "I felt as if a close relative had died," said Akol.

The worldwide response to the Ethiopia disaster was phenomenal, not only to World Vision, but to the whole humanitarian effort. Our Ethiopia budget grew from U.S. $2.3 million in 1984 to U.S. $43.4 million at the height of the emergency in 1986, plus 118,000 metric tons of food and supplies worth another U.S. $62 million.

This put enormous pressure on the organization, especially in Ethiopia, where the staff increased from under 100 to 3,650 during the crisis. Over 100 of these people were expatriate staff from other World Vision offices, many coming for short terms of three to six months.

In the midst of all this frenetic activity, our staff encountered the agony of people, day by day. Tony Atkins, who had first surveyed the needs, returned to Ethiopia to head our therapeutic feeding program. Tony was a medical doctor with long experience in Africa. He wrote this moving account in a letter on November 12, 1984 at Alamata in northern Ethiopia:

> The huge throng of mothers and children left the shelter with little noise and not much bustle. For those severely malnourished kids, and for their brothers and sisters, the late morning feeding session was ended.

> While waiting for the World Vision Ethiopia team to clear away the cups and plates I found a little bundle of dirty rags sagging against a corner post. Small enough to be an empty cloak, yet breathing and in fact asleep. When I nudged him awake he was neither startled nor upset. A worker called out to one of the departing mothers to collect

her son. Several women turned and seemed, almost as it were, to shrug and walk on.

Berhanu was his name. He did not know what they called his village, nor how far away it was. He could recall the very long walk over many days to reach Alamata. He told of his mother dying on the way, and how they all helped to bury her. He told of his father bringing them to the town and of their search for food. Then he would say no more.

Later in the day one of the security guards, employed to watch the main gate to the center, recognized Berhanu. It seems he and an even younger brother had been among the crowd outside the gates these many days past. Like all the others they had begged for food and pleaded for admission.

I expect they were judged to be not sufficiently malnourished to qualify for feeding. Nobody noticed there was no longer any adult looking out for them.

Had not Berhanu slipped through the gate that day, probably hiding behind the skirts of some mother selected to bring in her children for feeding, then he too would have disappeared and died with no one to notice the passing. Died like his mother, then his father, then his baby brother.

A lot of controversy developed around our Ethiopia program. Some saw World Vision operating like a fire brigade in dealing with relief problems. Some organizations criticized us for what they regarded as an aggressive and uncooperative style. A residue of problems had to be dealt with as the level of activity was drastically reduced after the worst of the emergency was over. All of this left a tarnished image of World Vision in the minds of many.

At the same time, the high quality of World Vision's nutritional program and the saving of hundreds of thousands of lives must not be under-estimated. In addition, our two aircraft provided a lifeline of communication to some of the worst-hit areas, carrying food, medicines, aid workers and journalists, both for World Vision and other organizations.

DEPENDENCY CRIPPLES PEOPLE

I once stood among hundreds of uprooted people in Southern Sudan, driven from their villages and livelihood by war. They were mostly naked, some clothed in a few shreds of bark or sacking. They waited patiently in long lines for the grain that would keep them from starving. Suddenly a Sudanese relief worker turned to me and shouted in pain and anger, "People should not have to live like this!"

Though emergency relief is necessary to save life, dependency on relief robs people of their dignity. Eventually they can lose the motivation to work for themselves. Entire countries can build their economies around relief aid, as in Mozambique.

Bruce Menser, director of World Vision's Sudan relief program, describes his approach to the problem:

At one of our Sudan relief/rehabilitation sites over the past year we have battled with the local authorities on the transition from relief to rehabilitation. But the dialogue was maintained and World Vision, working with the local community, has successfully stopped free relief distributions and moved to more of a market/bartering approach.

Today the same relief commodities are sold to farmers in exchange for their surplus food production. Other commodities are now sold to small community groups that specialize in tailoring, soap making and bicycle repair, and are able to produce products for introduction to the local market. World Vision is participating in the stimulus of the local economy. In the process people are happy to be working and producing their own products, enhancing household income and family security.

In some cases we are struggling to keep up with the community enthusiasm for these projects. In the Sudan war context it is truly exciting to see what can be done with even a small amount of stability.

The bartering/market approach also helps World Vision to maximize utilization of scarce resources as we reinvest sale proceeds back into funding for our project work. Other spinoffs include the more equitable and orderly distribution of resources throughout a wide geographical area. Local market mechanisms reach deep into the bush. Goods find their way to remote villages. Theft is reduced because goods now have personal value with the intrinsic respect of the marketplace. In the past we found that relief goods distributed freely inevitably led to chaos and corruption. There was never enough for everyone and the understanding prevailed that free goods belonged to everyone, so theft was common.

In Ethiopia and Mozambique the use of "agpaks" provided a simple and practical transition from relief to rehabilitation. Agpaks consist of tools, utensils and seeds cultivated for the particular conditions. Agricultural specialists explain how to use the kits and obtain the best results. As far as possible the items used are purchased locally.

T*HE* D*ESERT* I*S* F*ERTILE*

The old Ethiopian stood up to speak.

When we were so weak that we didn't even have the strength to bury our dead children, World Vision was here to help us bury them. When we were so weak that we couldn't even eat with a spoon, World Vision was here and fed us. When we finally gained enough strength so that we could return to our villages, World Vision gave us seeds and tools and encouraged us to go home and start again.

Going home to start again — is it really possible after what Ethiopia suffered. Yes it is! Ansokia Valley is living proof.

Located 200 miles northeast of Addis Ababa, Ansokia was a parched dust bowl during the famine of 1984. The people of that region were those the Western world saw on television screens in the agonies of starvation. In Ansokia, 60,000 of them clung to life by a thread, sustained only by World Vision's food brought to them on the backs of 300 camels over almost impassable terrain. I've travelled many times over these Ethiopian highlands, criss-crossed by enormous gorges and sheer escarpments, yet home to 88 percent of Ethiopia's population.

The costly food aid to Ansokia Valley was like putting a Band-Aid on a festering wound. While it kept most of the people alive, they had no future as things were. So World Vision's action right from the start was directed toward strategic development. It started with the people themselves.

Abdellah Ueman, who lived through the worst times, describes how the recovery started. "At first we just had to survive. Ideas totally stopped. Then the children started running around, playing. At that very moment we started thinking about how we can change this drought and turn this valley green. Then we started with AGPAKS and continued on."

Soil erosion was the worst problem. Experts say 1.6 billion tons of topsoil wash or blow away every year in Ethiopia. The country's once lush forests have almost disappeared. In Ansokia, for example, there was not a tree in sight, all having been used for fuel or construction. Even the roots that held the soil on the mountains had gone. But there were plenty of stones! So the people who were strong enough to work began building stone terracing.

A few lines here can't begin to trace the long road back to life for the people of Ansokia — it would take a whole book. The first steps were simple and slow, but they represented huge strides in courage for people who had barely escaped starvation. Eventually, seventeen peasant farmers' associations were organized; dams were built; over 200 kilometers of terracing was constructed; over five million trees were planted; the people organized in training programs, generating employment for thousands. Roads were improved and a bridge built to get goods in and out of the valley. It is a remarkable story of the greening of a valley that had the potential, not only to support its people, but to export food to other parts of the country.

Ethiopia Director Mulugeta Abebe writes, "The people of Ansokia Valley have sustained the development process. Each village has a development committee responsible for planning, implementing and managing the development programs. The community has also started to contribute resources for health posts, schools, flour mills and veterinary clinics." World Vision's role today is to strengthen local capacity and grass roots organizations.

What about the church?

Mulugeta explained that during the 1984 crisis, the personal lives and witness of the relief workers opened the minds and hearts of many people. As people came to faith, World Vision Ethiopia invited various churches to serve the valley. Today seven Christian communities are at work among the people as an integral part of the transformational development vision.

Ansokia provides a beautiful postscript to Tony Atkins' meeting with Berhanu described earlier in this chapter. Tony wrote in his diary two years later:

Visiting a magnificent integrated rural development project of World Vision in Ansokia I was welcomed as a guest by a crowd of excited orphan kids all singing and scampering around my legs, competing to clasp my fingers and catch my attention.

There in the group was Berhanu. He was instantly recognizable to me after such a moving introduction those years before. His hand was firmly held by an older girl, not family by blood but taught as they all were to care for the smaller ones. He was clean and well-nourished and healthy and smiling.

Then while I watched in wonder they sang songs of washed hands and clean faces and brushed teeth. And they sang of God's love for them.

Not all the large-scale projects were as successful as Ansokia. Over a three-year period (1985-87) World Vision started eleven large-scale programs in seven African countries. The emphasis was mainly on water resource development. "Large-scale" was defined as a project with a budget of more than $1 million, a time span of more than three years, a geographical scope greater than a single community, involving complex technical support and generally funded by one or a few large donors.

Later evaluation produced a classic list of typical problems related to large projects — limited community participation, narrow technical focus, top-down planning and control, unrealistic expectations, lack of local management and technical expertise. In later years important changes were made that led to redesign and recovery in many of the projects. New programs, especially in the field of community health, patterned on UNICEF's Child Survival concept, benefitted from earlier experiences. Several of these projects became models of successful large-scale development, particularly those in Louga, Senegal and the Child Survival Program in Zimbabwe.

A major review of child sponsorship in 1989 led by Peter McNee, the executive director of World Vision New Zealand, brought the best of our experience with large-scale programs into projects involving sponsored children. Called "Area Development Programs," this approach combined the benefits of scale with our best experience of transformational development.Tanzania provides one of the best examples of this new approach to sponsorship, illustrating how the spirit of partnership envisaged in internationalization operates at a community level as well as between nations. The excitement of Tanzanian colleague Reuben Shoo speaks for itself:

> So much has happened within a short space of time, that it appears as if a mighty glacier has suddenly melted, letting loose a fast-flowing current. Our programs have changed from church-based, single-village projects to community-based, Area Development Programs with direct World Vision assistance in management.

For the first time in our history, a community-based evaluation of World Vision programs was conducted and completed with stakeholders from the community itself, the church, World Vision Tanzania, government, World Vision Canada and World Vision International.

The Tanzania staff are more motivated and committed to their work. Capacity building is the order of the day and we have been transformed into a training institution, rated among the best community development facilitators in East Africa. Praise to the Lord.

With decentralization, more responsibility and accountability has been vested into the local districts. More decision-making takes place there and previous fears have been swept away that this system will not work! We are thirsting to share with others in the partnership what the Lord has done for us — the Tanzanian miracle — won't you invite us?

CORRECTING THE STEREOTYPE

Africa — historically called "darkest Africa" by Europeans because it was unknown, primitive, "uncivilized" — it is now known only too well. It is known by emaciated bodies, dying children with faces covered by flies, mothers whose thin babies suck at empty breasts, men stripped of dignity, unable to sustain themselves or their families. Bitter conflict, expenditure of scarce resources on guns and bullets, inter-tribal hatred, tyrants obsessed with lust for power. A continent described by one writer as being "in a free fall of despair."

The "civilized" world looks on with pity or judgment. But what is the legacy of the civilized West? Who but the civilized world tore Africa's young men and women from their villages, packed them in wretched slave ships, sold them into slavery? Who planted the flags of colonialism and sucked the economic blood from the continent? Who fostered war, peddled lethal weapons, used nations and peoples as pawns in deadly, real-life war games? This is the legacy of the "civilized" West.

But there is another legacy. It is the legacy of love, wrought through the sacrifice of brave men and women, missionary families, African martyrs. It is the legacy of the gospel. It is seen today in a vibrant church, which has demonstrated its faithfulness in the midst of violence and enriched the Christian church throughout the world by its witness. Where it has failed, as in Rwanda's recent holocaust, it grieves for its failure and seeks forgiveness and reconciliation.

I had a glimpse of the suffering church in Eritrea. I was told of an incident when a group of armed men burst into a church just as the service was about to start. A political figure in the congregation was shot dead and the people in the church were lined up against one wall and sprayed with machine gun fire. Twelve members of the church were imprisoned for eight months — four women and eight men. While in prison they shared their faith with other prisoners and many became Christians. After their release they continued to worship in houses and underground.

"We would meet every week in tunnels under the ground," one young man told me. "Sometimes we could not even talk. We would weep and weep and weep. God taught us so much."

Africa does not want the world's pity or charity. It needs sustained international solidarity in its struggle for a

better future. There is a new Africa in the making. We see it
taking shape in the miracle of South Africa. In many places
there is a new demand from ordinary people for accountability by their leaders. Some have called this a second
"wind of change." We need to correct the impression that
Africans can only receive, not give.

World Vision's vice president for Africa, James
Mageria, has a vision of Africa as "the continent of the 21st
century." This is not a shallow optimism. James knows the
realities. He is a survivor of the Mau Mau terror in Kenya,
having seen people killed before his eyes as a youth. His
vision is based on his faith in Jesus Christ and on the
capacity for sacrifice he sees within the Christian communities of Africa.

Africa is within itself a canvas in bold colors of the
whole world. Right now the dominant color is gray, signi-
fying the pervasive poverty and need of the continent. Great
blotches of red represent the spilt blood of conflict. But the
canvas is not complete. Rays of light hold the promise of a
new day. Patches of green reveal fresh life. Other bright
colors appear through the gray as the vitality and resourcefulness of Africa's people are released.

The former president of Tanzania, Mr. Julius
Nyerere, said to me, "God could have given us each a planet
of our own. But God put us together on this one." We are
one humanity. Africa's struggle is the world's struggle. God
calls us from the old paradigm of First World and Third
World to "One World."

We realize that there will always be a few skeptics, but they are the ones who keep us from falling asleep. They are the ones who play the role of "the loyal opposition." Working for unity has a price and this we have learned but, we have no choice, it is a command from our Lord himself.

— Eric Ram, World Vision Geneva

8

Global Player

"This morning the BBC broadcast the full story about famine in Ethiopia!" Relief Director Russ Kerr's voice over the phone was serious, but relieved. "It will be on television tonight! Thank God they've taken notice at last," he added.

For months World Vision and other agencies had tried in vain to get the media's attention drawn to starvation in Africa. Finally, thanks to Michael Buerk, a correspondent transported into the crisis area by our Twin Otter aircraft, the disaster hit the television network newscasts and the front pages of the world's newspapers.

Non-governmental organizations had always played a quiet, but effective, part in relief and development in Africa. In the 1985/86 Ethiopia crisis, however, they led the way, both in global advocacy and in the humanitarian response.

This role called for a high level of cooperation among individual agencies and a new era in relations with the United Nations and its specialized agencies.

We knew World Vision needed to do better in these relationships. So Tom Houston, in a major reorganization in April 1985, created a new international relations function to build relations with the United Nations system, the churches and other international organizations. He asked me to head the effort as vice president.

After ten years of field leadership through a time of tremendous growth and change, I was tired, much more tired than I realized. I also believed it was the right time for each of the major regions to have its own vice president, appointed from one of the countries within the region. This was part of Tom's plan and had been my own goal eventually. And I knew the new function was badly needed. I welcomed the move.

How Did Others See Us?

Father Thomas Stransky, former head of the Paulist Fathers, once said to me, "If World Vision does not speak for itself with truth and accuracy, others will speak of it from ignorance and distortion."

With this in mind I set out to knock on doors in Geneva, Rome, London, New York, Washington, Brussels and any other place where I could sit down with leaders of church denominations, the World Council of Churches, evangelical groups, UN agencies and other non-governmental organizations. My purpose was to tell our story and hear theirs.

World Vision had a reputation for "going it alone." This was not our intent. We did not deliberately adopt an uncooperative posture and certainly had no policy against cooperation. On the contrary, our position was always to share openly with others. But we often came across as arrogant. I remember the remark of Sri Lankan B.E. Fernando at the 1974 joint boards meeting in Thailand. "I perceive that World Vision is very good at giving," he said. "I think you need to learn how to receive."

Perhaps in our eagerness to get things done we would take short cuts and we repeatedly failed to consult as we should. Our Christian identity was often misinterpreted as narrow and fundamentalist. Because of our location in Southern California other international agencies assumed, wrongly, that we were an American organization. That in itself was no sin! However, it was an advantage in international work to distance oneself from any one dominant culture or nationality. All of these things added up to a pretty negative image in some circles.

The perceptions people had of World Vision started to come into focus. Some saw us as shallow, competitive, aggressive. Others admired our creative ideas and efficiency. Most saw us as big, powerful and rich. A few even thought we were evil. I tried first of all to listen, and then to understand why people saw us as they did.

Perceptions of World Vision were mostly of four types:

- *Some were true, or had grains of truth.* Where this truth was uncomfortable, we needed to examine ourselves with humility. We were not very good at that! Where the truth was favorable, we could take heart, be thankful and build on what was good.
- *Some were based on wrong or insufficient information.* These people didn't really know or understand us. Usually they had not met anyone

from World Vision, at least no one able to engage in serious dialogue on issues. A lot could be done to correct these impressions.

- *Some views arose from honest disagreement.* Talking face-to-face at least clarified the issues, revealed some common ground and built respect.
- *Some perceptions grew from prejudice.* These were the hardest to deal with. Prejudiced people did not and do not want to hear the truth and usually will not recognize it or accept it when they do.

Obviously not everyone would like us or agree with us. My purpose was not so much to win favor as to create understanding. To this end, I published a little booklet, *Understanding Who We Are,* in English, French and Spanish. I also began sharing with World Vision colleagues through newsletters, speeches and reports things we needed to learn from and about other organizations.

GETTING TO KNOW THE UN

We felt the need of establishing formal consultative relations with the United Nations in order to expand our working relationships with its specialized agencies. We went through the regular procedure for admission to Consultative Status with the Economic and Social Council of the UN. The final stage was a personal appearance before the 15-member non-governmental organization Committee of the Council. They asked questions for two hours before the vote, which had to be unanimous.

One question from the Nicaraguan delegate was interesting. He spoke in English; articulate, intense. "You are involved in development," he began. "Doesn't this create false satisfaction that diverts the people from the violent struggle for revolution?"

I replied that development in the best sense empowered people and gave them confidence to work for lasting change. We understood that frustration under unjust systems sometimes boiled over into violence, but in our view, violence was not an effective instrument for change. To keep people in poverty in order to fuel revolution was a form of political exploitation of the poor.

The many questions and comments were stimulating and I felt privileged to have the opportunity of presenting and defending our case. The vote was taken in the affirmative.

Our consultative status with the United Nations opened the way for more formal links with other UN agencies like the UN Children's Emergency Fund (UNICEF). We already had working relationships with the UN High Commissioner for Refugees, whom I had met with Stan Mooneyham during the Seasweep time. We also started the application process for official relations with the World Health Organization. This was more complicated, requiring the submission of a major health program spanning several years. The program would then be evaluated and a decision made. Eventually we were accepted and have enjoyed an excellent working relationship with WHO.

SHIFTING THE CENTER OF GRAVITY

Our California location isolated us to some degree from other agencies. Europe was the focal point for international humanitarian organizations and the World Vision Board accepted my proposal to locate an International

Liaison Office in Geneva. Fran and I moved there in November, 1987 and I was joined by Swiss colleague Suzanne Wavre, who had many years of World Vision experience in West and Southern Africa.

The most difficult and complex relationship we encountered was with the World Council of Churches. We touched the ecumenical movement at many points throughout the world and there was already a history of both positive and negative exchanges. As an Anglican layman and former YMCA leader, I was not a stranger to the movement. One of its founders, John R. Mott, was one of my heroes and I was strongly committed to church unity.

Yet in practice there were many difficulties. Most of these arose from statements about World Vision made by member churches of the World Council or affiliated national councils. Sometimes the problem was due more to personalities than to issues.

For example, the general secretary of the National Council of Churches in one of our support countries began our conversation with, "Tell me why we should be talking with World Vision?" A few refused to talk at all! But these were exceptions. In most cases I found people reasonable and open to dialogue. I had to keep in mind that the relationship with the ecumenical movement involved a vast network of people in both organizations all over the world.

It often seemed to me that the people I met could only think about the church in structural or institutional terms. Our philosophy of development led us away from institutional structures. We held that for sustainable development to be effective, ownership of the process has to be with the people, not with institutions or church structures. Insistence on working through such structures leads often to filters of bureaucracy that deprive the poor of benefit, while influential and powerful individuals within the structures engage in a power play of their own.

On the other hand, I had to face the fact that on the whole we had not done a good job of communicating, consulting and sharing with the full spectrum of churches at international, national and even local levels. There were specific issues of policy and practice that needed our attention too.

CIA CONNECTION?

One of the most harmful criticisms of World Vision over the years was the allegation of a connection with the CIA, the Central Intelligence Agency of the U. S. government. It all started in Cambodia in 1975. A group of journalists had seen World Vision's refugee housing project, which provided attractive, Cambodian-style houses for refugee families. The group also saw the medical program. Both these programs received substantial funding at that time from the U.S. Agency for International Development.

One member of the group of journalists, John Nakajima of Japan, asked if World Vision gave reports to the U.S. government. Our director replied that we gave the usual reports of the number of people housed or treated; the normal accounting for funds to any such government donor. Nakajima chose to give this casual and open reply a sinister interpretation in an article published by the East Asia Economic Review. He insinuated that we provide intelligence information to the United States government.

This nasty piece of misinformation was picked up at once by the wire services and flashed all over the world. Nakajima refused even to discuss the problem. He had his story and apparently was satisfied with what he had done.

Sometimes the story had a humorous twist. I once met with a group of church leaders in Ghana. The chairman in his welcome said, "We have a representative of the CIA with us today." I could hardly believe my ears and groaned inwardly. "Yes," he went on with a twinkle in his eye, "...Christians In Action!"

No shred of evidence has ever been produced by anyone at any time to support the CIA allegation. Not only that, but World Vision is on record as having opposed vigorously a suggestion by former U.S. President Gerald Ford that voluntary agencies and missions be regarded as a legitimate source of intelligence gathering.

ROUGH PLAY BY PAX CHRISTI

The Roman Catholic peace organization Pax Christi was responsible for the most damaging criticism ever levelled against World Vision. The issue centered on our work among Salvadoran refugees in Honduras. Following a shocking massacre of fleeing refugees by the Honduran and Salvadoran military on May 14, 1980, Pax Christi sent a delegation to Central America "as a sign of solidarity with the Christians and the religious organizations struggling for human rights." The delegation issued a report that included a denunciation of World Vision. We were accused of naming certain refugees with suspected guerrilla connections. This, supposedly, led to their deaths at the hands of the Honduran military. The report also painted World Vision as a sinister "Trojan Horse" for U.S. foreign policy in the region.

We were not aware of the Pax Christi mission or the report until articles started appearing in the press. Portions of the report had been leaked to the press before the report had even been seen by the Pax Christi executive. As a matter of fact, the report aroused a lot of controversy in the Roman

Catholic Church itself. A letter signed by 33 bishops and archbishops from 15 Latin American countries expressed regret for the Pax Christi report as being "an open injustice."

Since I was in charge of field operations at the time, I immediately commissioned a thorough internal investigation. A 50-page, detailed report examined every aspect of the program and dealt specifically with the Pax Christi allegations. No evidence was found that World Vision contributed to the deaths of the refugees or that we were in any way connected with U.S. government policy. The accusations had been based on rumor, innuendo and second-hand information, including press references to the old CIA story.

Our inquiry did reveal, however, that our relief response in Honduras was deficient in a number of critical areas. In its Summary the report stated:

> In trying to be apolitical in Honduras, we became frozen around inaction and security. We communicated by our stance that we favored the status quo, that we were not aligned with the defenders of the human rights of the refugees, and therefore, if not for them, against them. In the politicized climate, we were blind to the intensity of the human rights struggles and associated geo- political issues.

The findings of our investigation were a stern reminder to World Vision staff that even a small relief project, as this one was, could have profound repercussions if our own well-tested experience and policies were not followed. We took prompt action, including staff changes and a revision of relief policy. We also handed over the small project to a Honduran agency.

Meanwhile the publicity had gone worldwide. Newspapers in most countries where World Vision worked carried the story, which usually developed into a protracted debate in the press. A German newspaper published an article against World Vision based entirely on the report. World Vision in Europe then started legal action against both the newspaper and Pax Christi. Both actions were later dropped; the first because the newspaper went out of business and the second because of a technicality concerning Pax Christi's registration.

We began discussions with the Pax Christi international secretary in Antwerp, having sent a full copy of our investigation. Over the following six years World Vision pursued an active dialogue with Pax Christi at many levels, including a complete summary and correspondence about the whole situation to Pax Christi's president, Cardinal Franz Koenig of Vienna. Our letter to the Cardinal proposed a joint statement from both organizations, giving as the reason:

> References continue in the press worldwide to the Pax Christi report and its criticisms, not only of the refugee project, but of World Vision as an organization. The fact that there has been no retraction or qualifying statement from Pax Christi is regarded as an endorsement of its earlier criticism.

> Changes have been made in the policies of both organizations as a result of the controversy. It would be a constructive action to state this fact. Continued public reference to the conflict reflects badly on the character and aims of both organizations, which state their commitment to reconciliation and peace in the name and spirit of Jesus Christ.

No response. By this time I was in Geneva in the international relations portfolio. I proposed a formal dialogue between the senior leadership of both organizations. Instead, Pax Christi asked for more evidence that a problem existed!

The international secretary of Pax Christi did acknowledge to me privately that the allegations in their report were "unproven" and that, in his opinion, Pax Christi had a moral obligation to correct the injustice.

Eventually, at the request of Pax Christi, I presented another formal submission, this time for their Executive Committee. I pointed out that we had gone four times to Belgium, where Pax Christi's headquarters are located, and sent numerous papers, reports and correspondence. In the submission I wrote:

The statements about World Vision contain distortion, unsupported rumor and untruth. We do not ascribe malicious intent to this. We understand the conviction felt by the members of your mission in the climate of suffering they encountered. But we believe Pax Christi has a moral obligation to examine the facts concerning World Vision and to qualify the statements in the report accordingly.

Again, there was no response and has been none since. I believe that we cannot afford to behave toward each other and before the world like this. World Vision is not above criticism. No organization is. All have failed and made mistakes, because all are human institutions. But that does not excuse intolerance and lies.

How do we avoid these situations? By going to each other honestly with our concerns to clarify the facts, offering direct and constructive criticism. When organizations engaged in caring for others confront each other publicly or competitively, everyone is hurt, especially the poor. As an African proverb says, "When elephants fight, the grass gets trampled." I could not help but recall my experience as a young man in Australia when I had been struck by the comical irony of a leading newspaper article:

RIVAL 'PEACE' GROUPS CLASH

There were near riot scenes in Brisbane's Centenary Place today when more than 500 members of rival peace factions clashed for more than one and a half hours. Police were helpless to restrain the fighters as they yelled, brawled and punched each other in Brisbane's rowdiest-ever Sunday public forum.

I concluded that one of the best things needed in the worst times is a determination to widen the area of common ground, not destroy it.

STRATEGIC ALLIANCE HELPS CITIES

"You need a new vision for the city," said Dr. Ray Bakke, an experienced inner-city pastor from Chicago and coordinator of urban ministry for the Lausanne Committee for World Evangelization.

In collaboration with World Vision, Ray had conducted a series of urban consultations in the world's most crowded cities. The core of his approach was to encourage networking and coalitions among churches and organizations in the city, thereby generating vision and cooperation. I saw Ray in action in Mexico City and was impressed.

Great cities can stir the soul. That's how I remember feeling as a student when I first saw Australia's largest city, Sydney. I can still hear the muffled rumble in the distance as I approached the city by harbor ferry. I can see the dramatic skyline against the setting western sun. I picture the sparkling harbor dotted by a thousand sails.

But there's another side of Sydney, and I've seen that too. As I student youth worker I spent two years in the worst of Sydney's slums. I got to know its dingy streets and back alleys, its violence and misery, its sense of futility. Rat-infested hovels with earth floors where I sat with poor families 45 years ago are hard to reconcile with today's gleaming white Opera House. But that's the paradox of all big cities.

Slum clearance schemes in the West were supposed to change all that. Get rid of the slums, put up modern high-rise apartments, the argument went. I've seen those too, and all they accomplish is to condense the problems into a smaller space, packed with even more people.

Fran worked as a volunteer in an ecumenical visitation program in Melbourne's high-rise inner-city. Here she encountered the same human distress I found in Sydney. We volunteered together at a youth coffee house at the Church of All Nations in this area, and the pressure spilled over into our lives as Fran suffered a serious head injury one evening when drunken youths brawled nearby. We learned first-hand that the problems of big cities are common to all societies.

However, the rate of growth in the world's cities, especially those in poorer countries, is staggering. In 1950, when I was at work as a student in Sydney, there were only seven cities in the world with a population over five million. Only two of those cities were in the Two-thirds World. By 1985, 34 cities had passed the five million mark, 22 of them in poor countries. Calcutta, for example, is now a city of sixteen million people, equal to the entire urban population of Australia. Half-a-million people in Calcutta will live the whole of their lives, from birth to death, on the streets of that teeming city.

Before the mid-1980s, most of World Vision's development work was in rural areas. That is where most poor people lived, and we wanted to help stem the flow to the cities by tackling rural poverty. Also, rural communities were more suited to the development process. They were contained within more limited and defined boundaries; they usually had some form of leadership structure and they could be more readily introduced to the kind of participation and cooperation that makes up the fabric of development. In fact, the focus on the rural poor was one of the side effects of World Vision's historic shift from welfare to development. Most of our previous work among sponsored children, for example, had been in urban welfare- type institutions. As we implemented a development approach to sponsorship we found ourselves drawn more and more away from the cities.

The growing urban crisis was not altogether ignored. We had some good programs in city slums like the notorious Klong Toey district of Bangkok, but our approach was much the same as in rural communities, with limited success. We lacked a larger vision and strategy for the huge, crowded cities that were growing and multiplying at an alarming rate. Our strategic alliance with Ray Bakke and the Lausanne Movement became a springboard for a new global outreach.

Our first step was to bring an urban specialist on to the international team to help formulate and implement urban ministry strategies. It was Dr. Robert Linthicum who responded, coming with 26 years of experience in inner city churches, community organizations, housing and economic development.

Working with national colleagues throughout the world, Bob introduced principles of community organization specially suited to the urban context, and guided experimentation in the slums of 21 major cities in Asia, Latin America and Africa. The resulting projects have demonstrated clearly that the urban poor can be empowered to work together for change, with dramatic results.

I saw these results for myself in the once-fetid slum of Shastri Nagar, Madras, India's fourth-largest city. The most remarkable feature of the project was the energy and resourcefulness released in the people themselves at comparatively little cost to World Vision.

The people built their own school and employed the teacher. They organized themselves to have the city government pave all the roads, install street lights, put in sewer pipes and toilets. Local Associations were formed to obtain small loans for housing improvements and community-based businesses, with World Vision providing collateral. Because the one-year loans were repaid early, small loans are now available through the associations with no outside collateral. Remember, these people were the once-marginalized, rejected, powerless poor.

The women of Shastri Naga were the motivators, visionaries, energizers. The meeting of the Women's Association that I attended crackled with energy! The president of the Association said to me, "World Vision helped me see that this was our problem and we needed to find the solution."

Over a period of five years World Vision invested U.S. $35,000 for community organizing in Shastri Naga. This was used mostly to employ ten full-time community workers and provide training programs. But the community thus empowered generated nearly $1.5 million for community development from the government and other agencies. What other investment gives a return like that? Bob Linthicum described Shastri Naga as "a major work of liberation."

World Vision's Office of Urban Advance has become an active part of an international coalition of urban organizations and has contributed significantly to the literature of practical experience. Massive social problems like urban degeneration are too big for any one organization to handle. The only hope lies in strategic alliances that are both local and global.

CRISIS IN THE PARTNERSHIP

Our fledgling World Vision Partnership had survived ten years of global expansion, catastrophe in Africa and criticism from without. But a new peril loomed on our horizon. A season of discontent was evident within the organization itself.

World Vision's national directors from around the world gathered for the 1987 Directors' Conference in Sierra Madre, California. These were our executive leaders, responsible for World Vision's work in over sixty countries. Yet they felt they were not being heard by the international leadership. Nor were they hearing each other. It was like a chorus of the deaf.

Times of intense pain can become watershed learning experiences. Sierra Madre was like that. The directors, out of frustration, asked for a new agenda. Tom Houston as president wisely recognized the need to hear the concerns being expressed. The conference began to identify the most urgent needs of the organization. Tensions, contradictions and feelings were spilled out on the table. We talked "partnership" in World Vision, said the directors, but failed to live up to it in practice. The conference called for a process "to clarify our values in the light of experience so that a jointly-owned sense of identity and mission can emerge."

Could we negotiate this new bend in the road? As 1988 progressed, the executive committee of the International Board decided they needed to hear the views of World Vision's senior leadership. A meeting for this purpose was arranged, when fifteen executive leaders representing field, support and international operations came together for a week to review where we were as an organization, concluding with a joint session with the executive committee.

The group produced a statement describing "what is" and "what can be." They affirmed the vision of partnership embodied in the internationalization process and the general direction of the ministry, and then offered ideas for the future.

It would be unfair to lay blame for the tensions at the door of the president. The organization was still in the throes of growth and change. In many ways we were still discovering ourselves. Perhaps Tom could not embrace fully the changing style and mood of the time and the need for a shift outward in responsibility and authority. Despite Tom's evident gifts and personal integrity, there was a mismatch with the type of leadership the organization needed.

As Tom's term of office neared its conclusion at the end of 1988, he resigned as president. World Vision again faced the need for new leadership for the third time in less than ten years.

Part IV

From Symptoms To Causes

The Mission Statement and Core Values spell out the first things of our calling and our mission.

— Mac Bradshaw, World Vision Philippines

9

Getting To The Core

---

eneva, 14 September, 1988, 1:00 a.m.
"Who could be calling at this hour?" I mumbled to
Fran as the shrill ring woke us. As part of a global
family you get used to calls at odd hours, but this caller had
really mixed up the time zones!

"You'd better come over as quickly as you can,"
said the voice at the other end. "The board would like to
meet with you." It was Dr. Roberta Hestenes, chair of the
World Vision International Board. The next night I was in
California.

There was not time for a full search process for a
president, the board had decided. The immediate need was
space for healing, reviewing our global partnership and
finding a new sense of direction. The board would therefore
appoint an acting president for a maximum of two years.
This, in fact, had been the recommendation of the executive

leadership group in August. After hearing my ideas for the future, the board invited me to serve.

I called Fran in Geneva. Early that morning I had reflected on the Bible reading for the day in the Anglican lectionary, "The person who seeks to save his life will lose it, and the one who loses his life for my sake will find it. Whoever serves me must follow me, and where I am my servant will be also" (John 12:25,26). Fran and I knew that the path before us would be costly. And it was a price we would have to pay together. We had seen the demands of the organization and its global ministry on the lives of three World Vision presidents and their families. Yet we knew once again that God had called us. We agreed that I should accept the board's invitation.

The next night I looked out on the sleeping city from my hotel window. "What have I done?" I said to myself.

WHERE AM I GOING?

I had made clear to the board my view of the World Vision Partnership and the direction I intended to take. The organization could not work on the basis of heavy central control. Not only was this unworkable, it was not the way of the future in management leadership. You had to choose between a control-oriented, accounting-based organization and a people-oriented, training-based one. We had been trying to do both. The issue was not control or lack of control, but how and by whom control was exercised. I was committed to shared leadership within an agreed framework of values, mission, commitments and policies.

In a statement to the whole Partnership titled *Where Am I Going?,* I referred to this philosophy:

World Vision will be a professional, enlightened, efficient, humane organization. It will be an organization that nurtures a climate of creativity, in which people feel free to contribute, to develop ideas and have them taken seriously. Communication will be open rather than secretive; relationships more horizontal than vertical.

This philosophy was the fruit of my experience over many years in close relationship with support and field offices. I felt excited about the opportunity to share my vision as acting president. I believed this vision was in harmony with the direction the Partnership was moving, but in line with my declaration, I wanted to provide an opportunity for others in the Partnership to share their vision. The key was to create from our experience a frame of reference, a defined space within which creative people could move.

I had already been asked to lead the core values process at the next Directors' Conference. This was the first step; to clarify our sense of identity, to define the character of World Vision. Our actions would flow from our values. Revising the mission would come next. Finally, we would consider structure; how we worked together in global cooperation. These three — values, mission, structure — would be the essential parts of our frame of reference.

A MAP FOR THE JOURNEY

What are "core values?" They are underlying beliefs, fundamental principles, hidden attitudes that determine action. They come into play, as my American friends would say, where the rubber meets the road; or as we Australians phrase it, when it's a question of Sydney or the bush! In other words, when it comes down to ultimate decisions, basic actions, actual behavior. Core Values are buried deep.

As the World Vision Partnership grew to encompass over 60 national entities, we recognized a need to strengthen the sense of common understanding that bound us together as a ministering community. Our core values were our "commonality" — the things we held in common and struggled to preserve through any course of action.

For example, we might agree that people are more important than projects, that God is especially concerned for the welfare of the poor, that we are committed to protecting children. Such values need to be constantly reaffirmed, refined and applied to our ministry and service.

Organizations, like people, wear an exterior that may not be their true character. Reality is more interior than external. Core values are the true basis of a corporate culture.

I needed a process that would draw from our experience. Also there had to be ownership of the result by the whole organization, since values cannot be imposed or legislated. I began by asking every World Vision office to generate ideas from discussion with their staff on four questions:

- What are the particular values that drive World Vision?
- What are the values of the Kingdom of God?
- Where are we falling short?
- What should we try to become?

Everyone took the project seriously and sent in a huge amount of material. Fran and I went up to Zermatt, beneath the great spire of the Matterhorn, where I buried myself in all this raw data for several days, emerging only for a daily walk in the mountains. I developed a workbook as a tool for arriving at the core values and set off for the Directors' Conference in Australia.

In Sydney I spent a weekend with our younger daughter, Ros. When I showed her the result of my efforts, she said, "Dad, this is no good! You've done all the work for them." She had read the raw material and was excited by its richness. "You've got to get the conference participants into this material." So while I painted her apartment, she worked out a plan that was the key to the success of the core values process.

By the end of the conference we had drafted 95 percent of the Core Values document. We celebrated the work accomplished, discussed ideas for implementation and had prayers of thanksgiving.

The Core Values were adopted by the International Board in March 1990, and were signed by every participant at the World Vision Council meeting six months later. (See APPENDIX "B").

The adoption of the Core Values by the board also marked my appointment as the fifth president of World Vision International at the same meeting in March 1990. During the previous fifteen months stability had been restored, a spirit of healing was evident and there was a positive mood in the Partnership.

It had been a team effort. A combined board and staff review committee led by my Australian colleague, Harold Henderson, had done good work on our mission and structure.

My closest colleague and senior vice president, Dean Hirsch, had shared the challenge of getting things back on track. Loyal and dedicated, with an immense capacity for handling complex work, Dean had thrown his lot in with me when I invited him to join me 18 months earlier. Now we felt part of the burden was behind us, and looked forward to the task ahead.

Dean's positive attitude was a gift to me and to the organization. It also prompted some humor at times. Jim Canning, vice president of administration and finance, was our resident humorist. "Dean, you're so positive," Jim said one day, "that if you'd been captain of the *Titanic,* you'd have told everyone you had stopped to take on ice!"

The service commissioning me on June 15, 1990, was framed by the six Core Values. The six statements were illustrated by banners and I was called on to commit myself to each value, presented in turn by staff colleagues, an African child, a sponsor, a board chairman. The community of World Vision joined me in the act of commitment. So it is that these expressions of our corporate character have become etched into the life of World Vision. Our desire is that they should be not merely repeated words, but the facial features of our identity, so to speak, recognizable in World Vision people wherever they are.

Stan Mooneyham came to the Commissioning Service at my invitation and offered a most moving prayer. His departure from World Vision eight years earlier had been painful for everyone, but here at last there was healing. One year later, almost to the day, Stan died.

WHAT SHALL WE DO?

We were now ready to start on a new Mission Statement. Again I asked every office to contribute by telling their story; where had they come from, where were they now, where were they going? The stories were told by pictures, charts and drawings, hung all around the walls at the next Directors' Conference in Germany, 1990.

This was followed by written input gathered from staff, boards, project communities, donors, friends and critics of World Vision.

Working with the Core Group on Mission, we developed a first draft and began a process of interaction around the world by correspondence. It took 24 drafts before a statement emerged that defined World Vision as an "international partnership of Christians whose mission is to follow our Lord and Savior Jesus Christ in working with the poor and oppressed to promote human transformation, seek justice and bear witness to the good news of the Kingdom of God." We then enunciated and defined six specific goals of this holistic commitment.

The complete statement was finally adopted by the International Board in 1992 and ratified by the Council that same year in Antigua! Since then the process has continued by deepening our understanding of the Mission Statement and developing working policies for the six areas of action contained in it. (See Appendix C)

Has anything changed? That's the question! These documents were not intended to adorn the walls of offices, but to affect decisions and behavior. That takes time, especially in an organization with 6,000 staff members in over sixty countries. It's like changing course in a great ocean liner at full speed.

Both the Core Values and Mission Statement have taken hold throughout the organization and it is always encouraging to me to see them quoted and used as a kind of road map on the journey. Some examples from recent correspondence: "The Core Values and Mission Statement are the corner stones of the Partnership"(Taiwan); "The growing commitment of all national entities to the Core Values and Mission Statement is a powerful sign of change" (Cambodia); "We are more focused" (Tanzania). Bob Seiple, president of World Vision United States, summed it up, "Core Values are the glue that holds us together."

HOW SHALL WE WORK TOGETHER?

The third piece in the frame of reference is the Covenant of Partnership. Our institutional pilgrimage had taken us along a path toward a partnership of national entities held together by shared agreements, values and commitments rather than legal contracts or a controlling corporate center. At the same time we wanted an orderly structure and a clear basis of understanding. The Covenant was seen as a statement of accountability to each other, setting out the privileges and responsibilities of national member-entities of the World Vision family.

Since the Covenant is essentially an agreement between boards, it was drafted under the leadership of Jacques Daccord, chair of the Canadian Board. Once the form of the Covenant was agreed, it would be ratified by each national board. The draft was ready for the Antigua Council of 1992, where it was fully discussed and some changes suggested.

In presenting a Biblical concept of "covenant" to the Council, Australian board member and theologian, Noel Vose, said:

A fully Christian covenant is not legalistic, because it is not a contract. This does not mean that it is not binding, but the cords that bind are the cords of love. And in the last analysis, love is more binding than law, and grace is more binding than justice.

The Covenant has since been completed and ratified by all the national offices worldwide who make up the World Vision Partnership.

The final piece in the whole process that we launched ourselves on in 1988 was a review of our World

Vision structure and governance globally. Note again the order in this process — values, mission, commitments, structure. The process was designed that way. It's the same principle referred to earlier of taking one step, which yields experience and insight that allows a further step to be taken. By the time we reached the more difficult and controversial issues of governance and structure, a climate of trust and common understanding had developed as a base from which to work. The structural work is nearing completion as I write, led by the International Board chair, David Jenkin, and a small task force of nine women and men representing every continent.

Have we then at last got everything "right?" Of course not! We hope we have laid the basis for effective global action for at least the next 10 to 15 years, however.

Yet in another sense the process of renewal must continue. There is no permanent, static "right way." Philip Hunt, chief executive of World Vision Australia, points out that the core values were inherent in World Vision ten years before they were articulated; that the mission is not new, but a fresh statement of what has been evolving since the late 1970s; that there has been increased emphasis on the Partnership, although Stan Mooneyham's vision of "a different kind of international organization" is more than two decades old. Philip sees in this process the continual creative work of God. "I see more and more of the vision being realized every week," he said.

As I prepared to write this book, I invited colleagues all over the world to write to me with their thoughts, dreams and ideas about World Vision and their experience in ministry. To some degree I wanted this book to be "our story" as well as mine. I received scores of letters representing every office in the world. I've quoted from many of them and wish I could include them all.

These letters confirm what Philip Hunt said above. We have been drawn together around "a jointly-owned sense of identity and mission," in the words of the need expressed by the Sierra Madre Conference of 1987.

Lest it all sound too neat and tidy, I should add that the process of discernment and consensus-building in a large, diverse organization like World Vision is anything but tidy. To quote a good friend of mine and World Vision's, the process is often a "messy, sometimes conflictual, sometimes compromised corporate muddle out of which the good Lord somehow makes good decisions emerge!"

I believe we were guided through a critical transition process by the wisdom God had given to our World Vision community through our experience and reflection, and which we were able to share with each other to chart our path ahead.

When I requested input for the book from World Vision staff, the core values and mission statement appeared again and again in their responses as lynchpins for those working on the ground. One of the values most wholeheartedly supported was World Vision's policy on and commitment to justice. These were comments from people who labor in extreme situations, who see the realities. It is a tremendous encouragement to them to know that as well as fighting fires, World Vision is committed to tackling the fire-starters. The movement to deal with causes as well as symptoms of suffering is the third major shift in World Vision's journey.

A commitment to speaking the truth on an unpopular topic is to me an indicator that we are truly following Jesus Christ. We are addressing causes rather than just symptoms of poverty and oppression.

— Bill Warnock, World Vision Jerusalem

10

A Voice For The Voiceless

"Deafening silence" was the attitude ascribed by one observer to the world community when the Khmer Rouge slaughtered more than a million of their Cambodian countrymen in 1975. The whole world became guilty bystanders simply by their failure to speak up in protest.

Commitment to justice was the one entirely new element in the Mission Statement compared with earlier statements of purpose for World Vision. It was a shift in emphasis from dealing with symptoms to addressing causes. Not that this was altogether a new thought for us. Much work had been done behind the scenes in earlier years for the cause of justice. But it had not been a visible and formal part of our mission.

The movement toward justice as a World Vision objective began in 1981 when Stan Mooneyham asked board member John Rymer, Anglican Dean of Auckland, to study the issue. For John the study became a mission in life. He traveled to project communities and visited church leaders, including those at the Vatican and World Council of Churches. As a theologian he searched deeply into scripture. He headed a Justice and Reconciliation Committee of the International Board to involve other board members. All this led to the World Vision Board formally adopting a position on justice, based on John Rymer's extensive work.

At the same time, our work among the poor was taking us along the same path. In a conference at Merroo, Australia in 1982, field directors addressed the theme *World Vision in a Political and Social Context.* They shared stories of actual problems facing them. In one case study, a field director was asked to sign a statement of protest against atrocities committed by government troops. Another role play demonstrated how local security forces might exert pressure on a field director as a result of an article published by World Vision in a support country.

The conference worked through the issues in depth and formulated guidelines for action. In their conference statement, the field directors said:

Our starting point is the justice of God as recorded in Micah 6:8, "This is what the Lord asks of you: only this, to act justly, to love mercy, and to walk humbly with your God."

Field directors acknowledge that a diversity of social and political issues seriously impacts the lives of the poor. We dare not adopt a naive attitude by addressing ourselves in our development process solely to the symptoms of injustice and sin. A critical understanding of reality is necessary as we carefully consider basic causes of the plight of the poor.

There will be a continual struggle as we seek to hold in tension integrity and expediency. We must beware of using injustice to bring about justice.

The Merroo conference was a watershed in many ways. It was the most serious effort we had ever made to hear our field colleagues in a way that enabled their voices to help shape the policies and direction of the whole organization. Their statement on justice was loud and clear; progression from relief to development, then to empowerment of the poor led inevitably to the call for justice.

GOD IS A JUST GOD

Some in World Vision were uncomfortable with this direction, especially when it came to public advocacy. "We must not become political," they would say. It was always my position that World Vision does not have a political agenda. We have a Christian and humanitarian agenda. But the political consequences of that agenda cannot and must not be avoided.

The call for justice is a Biblical imperative, as John Rymer made clear in his studies. The central theme of both the Core Values and Mission Statement is "following Jesus." To follow Jesus takes us immediately into a conflict zone with forces that deny people their basic human dignity.

Take the case of Jesus' healing of a man with a "withered hand" recorded in Mark, Chapter 3. The scene is a crowded synagogue on the Sabbath. News of Jesus had spread over the whole region. Everyone is looking for him — the sick, the deformed, the depressed, the demented, the curious.

The enemies of Jesus are there too. It has not taken long for opposition to be aroused toward this teacher who speaks as no other has spoken. His opponents may even have put the man with the crippled hand there, in the front row. Mark says "they were looking for a reason to accuse Jesus, so they watched him closely to see if he would heal the man on the Sabbath."

Jesus knows all this. For lots of reasons it would have been prudent to avoid a show-down with the authorities. Note that he is dealing here not only with religious authority, but with political power. Under the terms of the Roman occupation, the Sanhedrin administered Jewish affairs. He could have said quietly to the man, "I've noticed your hand, but it's a bit awkward to do anything about it here. Come and see me tomorrow and I'll take a look at it."

Instead, Jesus makes a big issue of the encounter. "Stand up here in front of everyone," he says to the man.

Then he throws out a challenge to the crowd, "Which is lawful on the Sabbath; to do good or to do evil, to save life or to kill?"

His enemies are silenced. Then Jesus, "deeply hurt by their inhumanity, looked with anger on the faces surrounding him."

Turning to the man standing there he says, "Stretch out your hand." And it is completely restored. The Pharisees go out immediately and conspire to destroy Jesus.

It is clear in this narrative that the act of healing, though beautiful in itself, is not the only issue, or perhaps even the central one. Jesus deliberately chose to confront an unjust, oppressive system that put man's religious rules before people and denied the very character of God. And he put his life on the line to do it.

To have developed a policy was one thing, but where and how to put it into practice? This was the real test for World Vision as we took a controversial new direction, strongly felt and supported by the Partnership, but as yet untried, a new road in the journey. Should World Vision decide to take on this role, we must be prepared to put ourselves on the line, to face criticism from outside and from within. Hunger, drought, disaster — these we knew, and had years of experience with. But behind these familiar adversaries we began to see the shadows of the real enemies of humanity — greed, power, hate — and to probe the darkness.

CHILDREN AND JUSTICE

Children have always been at the center of World Vision's work. All over the world, children's voices are the last to be heard, the first to be silenced. Who has not heard about a case of child abuse and been appalled? Yet these stories are too common, even in our own backyards. It is natural, then, that we should be a voice for them when they are neglected, abused and deprived. Sueli Duarte Costa de Melo of World Vision Brazil speaks eloquently for Brazil's marginalized children:

> I'm one of the thousands
> Of needy children in Brazil.
> Without dreams, I live the present.
> My life is such a sad story,
> Without dreams, tales or enchantments.
> I mean a suffering people,
> That dies due to lack of bread.

I give you my little heart and ask you,
"Give me your love.
Come and take part in this story,
Take part in the solution.
This is transforming stone into bread;
It's overflowing the desert
With living water."

A little heart
Desirous for love, how many times
I've been crying and shouting?

But nobody listens;
I'm a silent cry.

Even when you hear that cry, acting on it puts you on a long, hard road on which you meet many adversaries. It is not enough only to speak or issue statements. That's the easy part.

A child enters the world with unquestioning trust. It is totally defenseless and powerless, depending completely on adults for protection and care. It is at the mercy of the world around it. Jesus took children seriously. "Receive a child, receive me," he said. And he set his face sternly against those who would harm a child. He warned that anyone who lays a careless, exploitive or destructive hand on a child does something so terrible as to deserve being banished from the earth. We must not let the cry of poverty's children remain a silent cry.

Here is a little girl, Noi (not her real name), only 14 years old, living with her parents in a hill village of northern Thailand. Life here is hard and the future bleak for this family of a subsistence farmer. So these poor rural districts facing chronic drought have become targets for Thailand's notorious sex industry, with its deceptive promise of quick money and an attractive life in the city. Pressure is put on young girls to "provide" for their parents by selling the only commodity they possess — themselves. The younger the girl, the less chance she has of being already infected with the AIDS virus, and the more appealing to "customers."

Though Noi had a World Vision sponsor, the lure of the city and the hope of improving the lot of her family led to her fateful decision to leave home. Her parents received an "advance" of 10,000 baht (U.S. $400) for their daughter, who set off for Chonburi, a booming city on Thailand's east coast. Once there, a relative introduced her to the "trade."

The whole sickly business is highly organized, ruthless and unspeakably evil. Once trapped into prostitution, these children become the property of pimps and criminals. Many become infected with HIV and are eventually turned out on the street, physically and emotionally destroyed.

Fortunately for Noi, her World Vision sponsor was at the time working in Thailand with the Christian organization, Youth With A Mission. Just days after she had left her village, Noi's sponsor requested a meeting with her. When the World Vision office in Bangkok began making arrangements, they were told by the project leader that Noi had left the program a few days earlier. They sensed something was wrong. Since the sponsorship program requires follow-up with children who drop out, the staff arranged a visit with the parents, inviting the sponsor to come. The visit confirmed their suspicions — Noi had gone to a brothel, not a restaurant in Chonburi as they had been told.

There was no time to lose! Within three days World Vision's staff in Chonburi found Noi and managed to speak to her, a dangerous game for all concerned, since many young girls are killed by their pimps for trying to escape. Noi confided that she wanted to get out of the brothel and go back to school. How much do you pay for the life of a child? In this case, 16,000 baht (about $640) secured the release of Noi.

Eventually, operators of brothels like the one Noi was in need to be brought to justice. In Noi's case, our main concern was the safety of the child. The enactment and enforcement of protective law is a longer term goal. Noi is now in a residential Christian home for young women and girls in Bangkok. She is a good student in her second year of secondary school and has gained strength from her new faith in Jesus Christ. Thanks to timely action by the World Vision team and her sponsor, Noi has tested negative for the dreaded HIV virus.

Noi's case illustrates different levels of advocacy. Local staff play a key role, while child sponsorship offers a dimension usually overlooked by its critics; that is, a partnership of caring that can literally save the life of a child.

As part of our campaign against child exploitation, World Vision New Zealand encouraged all its sponsors of Thai children to write to the Government of Thailand urging action to protect children. I met personally with the Prime Minister to thank him for recent efforts to curb exploitation and to assure him of World Vision's support. During our conversation the Prime Minister rightly pointed out that child abuse is an international problem, not peculiar to Thailand. At the same time he assured me of his government's serious commitment to turn the situation around.

THE OLDEST OPPRESSION IN THE WORLD

Another justice issue for World Vision involves women.

"The oppression of women," wrote Bishop Mortimer Arias of Bolivia, "is the oldest oppression in the world." Women have for centuries been conditioned to low self-esteem. Men have used their physical strength and economic advantage to subordinate women and assert their own assumed superiority.

From the day they are born, female children enter a world that is at best prejudiced against them, and at worst dangerously hostile. In some societies their gender alone brings immediate or early death. They are unwanted, unwelcomed and unaccepted. Multitudes of girl children do not have the same access to education, health care or vocational opportunity as boys. In some societies their bodies are painfully mutilated by female circumcision. Vast numbers are forced into exploitive relationships with no regard for their wishes or welfare. The sexual abuse of young girls through prostitution is a multi-billion dollar international industry. No country or society is innocent of these crimes against women.

In World Vision the awareness of the needs of women has been slow in coming, at least in a way that produced a major change in policy and strategy. This is not to say that we have not done very good things in countless places over a long period to affirm the dignity of women and release their gifts. We have seen that women are the prime movers in development. They are closer to reality than men. They face the daily necessity of feeding children, providing clothing, creating a home and nursing the sick. While men often walk away from problems, women face right into them. However, they are traditionally denied participation in the management and control of the development process.

There comes a point where organizational commitment to an issue has to be strengthened. If we were serious about promoting justice, the question of women in development and leadership had to be given more deliberate attention.

At the 1989 International Council, sociologist Joan Levett, a former member of the Australian Board and at that time on the Latin America staff, spoke on behalf of women.

"We must make real our declared commitment by enabling women to participate in all phases of development and at all levels of management," she said. Joan's recommendation to create a formal Commission on Women in Development and Leadership won unanimous approval from the Council.

World Vision Canada vice president, Linda Tripp, chaired the Commission. She describes her experience in Ghana as she saw both the need and potential for work among women:

I was visiting a women's project in a slum called Labadi, in the heart of Accra, Ghana. The women in this community were the most abused and marginalized in the community. They each had several children, but had been terribly abused sexually, physically and emotionally by their husbands and other men.

Alice Yerenki of the Ghana staff trained the women in skills that would help them earn an income and lift them out of squalor. Starting at 5 a.m. they worked all morning to produce their products. Then in the afternoon they sold their wares and pooled resources.

These women could not read or write, but with Alice's help they learned to organize themselves. They set strict rules for membership and participation. In determining how to use their earnings, they ensured that the most needy were assisted first. By the time I visited the project they had all their children in school, with uniforms and books purchased and school fees paid. Their next plan was to buy a grinding mill, which would become another source of income for the group.

Every Thursday they had a project meeting, one of which I was invited to attend. They asked me to speak, but I knew they had far more to teach me than I had to give them. So after bringing greetings, I said, "Please imagine that I have a very large basket. Please tell me your stories and put them into my basket, so that I can carry them back to my country and share them with the people of Canada, who will hear you, stand with you and support you."

One by one they told of betrayal, disappointment, abuse and abandonment. Then one woman rose. She was only in her early twenties, but looked old because of what she had suffered. She told me how she had been raped, beaten and exploited by various men in her life. She was forced to prostitute herself in order to feed her children. The only thing that kept her from suicide was her love for her children.

Then she told how Alice Yerenki came and talked about change, about hope, about a chance to be better. At first she did not believe Alice. Her life had been full of false promises, shattered dreams. Hope was too painful to endure. But Alice persisted.

She said she began to feel a small seed take root deep inside her. And finally she decided to risk hope one last time.

Since joining the program, she discovered that she was capable of learning a skill and earning money. She has learned that God loved her in a deep and personal way.

Then with tears streaming down her face, a face that was scarred and broken, she said, "Now I know that when God looks at me, he sees a beautiful flower."

Changing attitudes and behavior that have profound historical, cultural, social and religious roots is slow and difficult. The Commission did excellent work, including extensive theological reflection. They recommended new policy that was adopted by the World Vision Board and affirmed at the 1992 Council in Antigua, Guatemala.

But policy is not action — it merely points the way for action. The real test of how serious we are about the role of women in development and leadership is the attitudes, decisions and actions that prevail wherever World Vision people do their work. We face that test every day.

Joan Levett later became the first woman to serve as a vice president of World Vision International. She died a few days before I wrote these words, actively working almost to the end of her life despite her long illness. Part of Joan's responsibility was helping World Vision people around the world to implement the new policy, but she was disappointed by the slow progress. Our best memorial to Joan would be to bring the policy to life. That would please her, and it would please our Creator.

Cambodia – A Case Study In Advocacy

The previous cases illustrate advocacy in the context of World Vision projects and policies — the work we already do and the way we work with people, specifically women and children. While small beginnings may have lasting effects as we shall see later, power all too often rests with the "decision makers," governments and bureaucracies of the world. Could World Vision speak for people among the real powerbrokers, in the corridors of power? We decided to speak on the political stage over Cambodia — a country broken, left, but not forgotten in the hearts of many World Vision staff. Here we had a chance to make a real difference, to leave a lasting legacy.

In 1975 the world had stood by silently while the Khmer Rouge butchered over a million of its own people. Yet the smiling face of Khmer Rouge deputy leader Khieu Samphan continued to represent Cambodia in the United Nations nearly 15 years later. This was far more than irony. It had the effect of isolating the six million survivors from international assistance, while supporting the murderers. It was a monstrous injustice. In moral terms I regarded it as an international crime.

I decided therefore to speak out publicly on the issue in Australia in November, 1989. Why then? Why World Vision?

- *First, we had a background of knowledge and involvement.* We had earned the right to speak. We had worked in the country for over 20 years and were the largest non-governmental organization there. Over 100 of our staff had died under the Khmer Rouge. We had consistently called for a change in international policy and had pressed the Hun Sen Government to grant religious freedom. I had personally been close to the situation for the full 20 years.

- *The cause was just and urgent.* Over one million Cambodians had died under the Khmer Rouge, including most of its educated, trained people. Yet Cambodia had no access to international aid because of the position taken by the majority of UN member nations. It was a stricken, desperate land.

- *Key people were consulted.* I discussed the issue with support country directors, who needed a clear World Vision position. I visited Cambodia to consult fully with staff on the ground and met diplomats in Geneva, Hanoi, Phnom Penh and Bangkok to gain perspective.

- *Australia provided an ideal public platform.* Chief executive Philip Hunt had invited me to come to Australia, where World Vision's high profile guaranteed media interest, especially as the issue was already getting a lot of publicity. Australian policy on Cambodia was under pressure and as an Australian citizen I could speak freely to my own government in my own country. There was a real chance of making a difference.

- *It was a unique moment in time.* There was mounting concern that the Khmer Rouge might return to power following the Vietnamese military withdrawal a few weeks earlier. I could be in Cambodia on the very day the UN vote on Cambodia's seat in the General Assembly was taken and issue a statement from there. The Hun Sen Government was more open to change; a good time to call for change in world opinion, as well as to press home our advocacy for recognizing the church in Cambodia. I also learned that a powerful documentary, which had already caused a shift in British policy, was to be shown nation-wide on Australian television. We timed my visit for that day.

Our plan worked. In Cambodia I issued a statement from the infamous Tuol Sleng prison where 20,000 intellectuals were tortured and executed. I made the statement on the day of the UN vote, when the Khmer Rouge were returned to the Cambodian seat.

Cambodia Director Glenn Beckwith and Asia Vice President Watt Santatiwat helped me draft a clear World Vision position on Cambodia. Media Director Glenda Orland and her team in Australia set up a press conference, followed by a packed schedule of radio and television interviews.

Two days later, the Australian Foreign Minister announced a change in Australia's position and offered a fresh proposal to declare the Cambodia seat at the UN vacant and work toward a peaceful solution during which the UN would provide an interim administration in Cambodia. It was what we had called for. It would be arrogant and untrue for us to claim credit for this. But there is little doubt that our advocacy influenced the course of events. "Following a public outcry...," was the way the press prefaced the Foreign Minister's announcement.

The UN Security Council accepted Australia's proposal, which led to free elections in Cambodia in 1993. The Hun Sen government soon after accorded freedom to all religions and the church was once again able to meet for worship.

It has never been our policy to advocate one political party over another, or to try to undermine political structures. Those issues belong entirely with the people. But we do stand ready to speak and work on behalf of people under oppression.

If done strategically, as in the Cambodia case, advocacy can help bring justice to a whole nation. Or the cause may be one person, one family, one community.

THE VOICE OF THE POOR

The voice for justice does not have to be the president's voice, or even that of World Vision. The voice of the people themselves makes the most authentic and powerful statement, as in Yamaranguila, Honduras.

Once the largest ethnic group in Honduras, the Lenca people were driven from their fertile valleys, exploited and humiliated, and forced to live in grinding poverty in isolated hills and mountains. Even there, they faced the loss of their dearest possession — their remaining land.

Like many indigenous peoples, the Lencas regard the land as far more than property. It is their sacred heritage, beyond price. But to the commercial sawmill that operated in the district the land represented only profit. Forty years of relentless logging in the Yamaranguila area threatened to destroy the environment on which the Lencas depended for their existence.

A few concerned leaders began a struggle in defense of the land. But when they appealed to the authorities that no more timber be cut, they were beaten and imprisoned.

Meanwhile, World Vision had begun working in the community through a child sponsorship program. Staff member Romualdo Rodriguez, who is originally from Yamaranguila, recalls the early days in 1987:

> We built a job training center. As the people started using the new technologies, they saw an increase in productivity. We began a process of reflection, thinking about our activities and the environment. It became clear to us that while we were striving to protect the environment, others wanted to destroy it.

World Vision organized 38 peasant farmer groups, who formed an Environmental Committee and made an urgent appeal for better land management policies. This led to some changes in Honduran law to protect the environment. But the logging company ignored the new laws and marked 800 more trees for felling in an area vital for wind protection and water conservation. The Environmental Committee saved the trees by pressing for the application of the new laws.

But the real battle still lay ahead — the closure of the sawmill. Jose Hector Rodriguez of the Environmental Committee explains why.

> It became increasingly clear that the forest was being destroyed. There was a shortage of water and oxygen. The climate was growing hotter and heavier. We wrote to the authorities asking that they put a stop to logging. Our purpose was to defend the right that belongs to us historically and constitutionally.

Death threats were made against the committee members. They were branded communists, guerrillas, saboteurs. The committee replied,

> Those of us who love the truth will not flee. Honduras needs people who think, people with a

vision. We are called to leave future generations a green Honduras, a Honduras with enough water.

Many other grass roots organizations joined the struggle. Eventually their unified voices became difficult to ignore and impossible to silence. The churches became involved too:

Nature was the first thing God created. If we as the church do not care for it, nobody will. We must care for it and protect it, because it is our very life.

When their cause fell on deaf ears, even those of the Minister for Justice, the people organized a March for Life with World Vision's help. Eventually they won an important victory. The community leaders signed an agreement with the government that creates reserves where no logging is permitted, establishes communally-owned lands where only the community groups may cut timber, and permits the people to start reforestation in previously cleared areas. The sawmill may not take timber from the Yaramanguila district. The people have decided to organize small-scale hand sawmills that will utilize wood as necessary, provide employment and protect the forest.

World Vision's Romualdo Rodriguez commented, "This is really a grass roots movement. World Vision helped a great deal through training and consciousness-raising, but our role in all these events has been quite limited. This is significant, because it shows that the people can sustain their efforts."

It is hard to imagine the courage it takes for powerless people to confront authority, especially hostile authority. Yet through their struggle for the land, the people of Yaramanguila have discovered that they have the resources for success. And most are within themselves.

In The Corridors Of Power

The World Bank is the largest institution concerned with Third World development — and the most controversial. With the help of my U.S. colleague in Washington, D.C., Tom Getman, I went to the Bank in 1986. I spent two days with senior officials of the Bank to understand their policies and structure and to see if some form of joint work was desirable and possible. In a report to the World Vision Partnership I wrote:

> The Bank appears to be open to dialogue and cooperation with non-governmental organizations. World Vision, because of its size and range of project work, is well-positioned to respond to this opportunity and the Bank was highly complimentary in its feedback from my visit. If a connection can be made with non-governmental organizations like World Vision, which are working from 'the underside of poverty,' I think there can be better participation by the poor, advocacy within the Bank for the interests of the poor and the possibility of addressing some of the social impacts of Bank policies which are largely ignored at present.

During the visit I began discussions with one of the Bank's public health officers, Dr. Vulimiri Jagdish, about a possible health project in Africa. As a result of excellent work by World Vision's Washington Office and our Africa staff, a major program with funding from the World Bank began in 1990.

The program was in Uganda, its purpose to help communities care for orphans whose parents had died of AIDS, and to build AIDS awareness through education. It was a small project for the Bank — U.S. $15 million — but a big one for us! World Vision contributed U.S. $2.5

million, so we had a definite stake in the outcome. This was a pioneering experiment, a three-way partnership between the World Bank, the Government of Uganda and World Vision. As the project got under way, I went to Uganda to see for myself.

Uganda. Once called the Pearl of Africa, its heart was torn out by the dictator Idi Amin. Then the scourge of AIDS added tragedy to tragedy. It is estimated that 10 per cent of the entire population of Uganda is infected with the deadly virus.

My visit took me to the Rakai district of Southwest Uganda, one of four districts served by the program. Everywhere I went in Rakai the simple houses of the people were surrounded by little mounds of earth; the graves of those who had died from the dreaded disease, called "slim" in Uganda, because its victims waste away to skin and bone.

Imagine you are with me as I talk with one sad family where death hangs heavily over the little group seated on stools outside their thatched house. A fourteen-year-old girl with an intelligent, but sad, face explains that her father died a few months earlier. Her mother, who is with us in the group, is dying too. Her uncle, also in the group, is near death. Soon the only surviving adult will be her grandmother, seated with us. Around us lie the familiar mounds of earth.

"What is your name?" I ask.

"My names are Jane Namuwawu," she says, and writes it down for me. I learn that she had had to drop out of school because she had no suitable clothes and cannot afford the school fees.

Then Jane begins to cry. Tears stream down her face and I wonder what I have said to distress her. Later I ask my colleague, Moses Dombo, what the problem was. He repeats what Jane had said to him in the local dialect.

"Who are you people?" she had asked. "When my father died I thought my life had ended. Now it's as if my father has come back."

Within a few months Jane was an orphan. Fran and I now have the privilege of sponsoring her and providing educational support for Jane and her sister Harriet. They are both doing well and as I write these words, I have a letter from Jane in front of me received only this week. She says she is praying for me, and I believe it. I pray for her too. She has described her daily life at school and in the community. It is a long letter that she signs as "your loving daughter." Thank God there is hope for Jane and Harriet. In fact, a new generation of young people intensely aware of the facts about AIDS, and committed by the grace of God to a disciplined, responsible life is the only hope for the nation's future.

Three months after my visit to Rakai, I called on the president of the World Bank, Mr. Barber Conable. We talked about the project and the benefits of our collaboration, especially in terms of people-participation. Then I told him about Jane.

"Mr. Conable," I said, "As you lead this huge institution from your office here in Washington, I hope you will remember Jane and know that your decisions affect the lives of real people like her."

Together with other voluntary organizations, World Vision has worked actively to make a constructive contribution to Bank policy and practice. Ugandan Joe Muwonge of our Washington, D.C. office and Stephen Commins from my office have served on many joint Bank/non-governmental organization committees. We have seen real changes in the Bank's burdensome procedures, including greater flexibility and a willingness to engage in serious discussion with the voluntary sector about policy and operational practice. We have tried to move the focus of the Bank out of Washington and into Africa to allow African non-governmental organizations to sit at the table with senior Bank staff and be heard.

The voice for justice need not be shrill or strident. Usually it can be heard better when it is the voice of reason and compassion. It may be a lonely voice, unpopular, rejected, misunderstood. No matter. We must not be silent or passive before evil, even if only the stones listen.

There are some men for whom a tree has no reality until they think of cutting it down, for whom an animal has no value until it enters the slaughterhouse, men who never look at anything until they decide to abuse it and who never even notice what they do not want to destroy.

— Thomas Merton

11

War Is Hell

In Rwanda I visited a center south of Kigali where many hundreds of children were receiving medical care and temporary shelter. The youngest and weakest children were lying on mattresses on the concrete floor of a very large room; perhaps two hundred children. I came upon one who seemed somehow totally alone. She was only three or four years old, lying quite still. She had little strength left. Her eyes were dull, uncomprehending. She was near death.

I could not walk away, but I did not know what to do. There seemed nothing anyone could do. So I simply lay down near her and stroked her head. I held her tiny hand in mine. She was wearing a pink playsuit and through my tears I noticed the words "Baby Girl" embroidered on the front. I thought of my own two daughters when they were little. I remembered the care with which Fran and I nurtured the tender new lives God had entrusted to us. Now here was this little one with no one near. Closing my eyes, I prayed that she would be enfolded in God's loving presence. I wanted to convey to her some feeling of love and comfort as her life slipped away.

"Baby Girl" was a symbol for me of the obscenity of war, of the lust for power that drives it, the hatred that fuels it, the greed that exploits it. This is what war did. I rose convinced that we must find ways to shield these most helpless of all war's victims to our utmost capacity, working in cooperation with other agencies that had the same concern.

Children under five are the most numerous and severely affected victims of today's armed conflict. Their plight is part of the very soul of World Vision. It's how we began.

When I learned in July 1994 that an estimated 50,000 children (later revised to 100,000 by UNICEF) were orphaned in Rwanda as a result of the massacres, their desolation gripped my heart. They had nowhere to go and no one to be with. They were nobody's children. I was determined to mount a fresh World Vision initiative for children of war.

The Children of War program first of all gives special attention to lost, abandoned or orphan children, technically called "unaccompanied minors." Their first need is survival. That means shelter, food, medical care and protection.

Secondly, the task is to return them to their family or community and ensure that they are in safe hands.

Third, the inner suffering of children needs careful and professional counseling. They have a basic need to speak about what they have seen and experienced, to work through the trauma with a sensitive, trained adult.

I am sickened by war. For 27 years I have walked among its victims, witnessed its savagery, seen its wanton destruction.

For me the city of Mostar in the former Yugoslavia said it all.

A once beautiful and historic city now pounded to rubble. A priceless medieval library completely destroyed. Overwhelming human misery. Broken buildings, broken roads, broken lives, broken dreams. After two days amidst this carnage in November 1993, I lay awake one night in the freezing cold listening to the pounding of artillery fire only 150 yards away. Sounds of a different kind indicated incoming shells. Machine-gun and rifle fire were constant. Without heating of any kind, I had tried to warm my hands over a candle I had brought with me. Now I thought of the soldiers out all night in the unbearable cold. I thought of men, women and children who would be victims of those rounds in the middle of the black, freezing night; their homes ruined, their bodies torn, their hopes shattered. The evil and futility of it swept over me; those responsible for it filled me with loathing.

GOODBYE, MY VILLAGE

Ghada Daabous was 18 years old when I met her in Lebanon. The bombing of her village began when she was three. All her living memories are of war. When she was seven, a bomb exploded near her as she ran to her church for protection. The blast hurled her against the wall, gashing her right cheek severely. For nearly a year she could not speak; her tongue would not move. Gradually the condition improved.

At five, Ghada started keeping a record of her thoughts in the form of drawings. The book was destroyed in one of the bombings, but she started another when she was eleven. I looked through her book, moved by her stories and drawings. Ghada's book chronicles the battering of her beloved village and the suffering of its people. It tells how she became accustomed to death and injury. For days on end she would huddle with others in the church, sometimes going without food for days. She saw a man decapitated. She saw a woman burned to death. She remembers being lined up against a wall with other children by soldiers who threatened to kill them and then fired machine guns into the wall above their heads. She remembers the harvest fields ablaze from incendiary bombs.

"We learned how to save ourselves," she told me. "The war made me hard. In the end I didn't cry or shout. I kept my feelings inside of me. But I would get headaches. The war made me older than my age."

Ghada could tell when an oncoming plane was preparing to attack. "The voice of the engine would change," she recalls.

During these years Ghada changed school seven times as the buildings were destroyed one by one. "The war destroyed not only our houses, but our lives," she said.

Ghada somehow keeps a cheerful spirit despite her suffering. "We must laugh. Let us be happy. It is better to be cheerful than angry. We must love. Love is the normal life."

A poignant poem, taken from her book of memories, reveals the destructive force of war in the world of a child:

Goodbye my village on the hill
Like a king sitting on his throne.
Goodbye O destroyed houses,
And ashes of every home.
Goodbye O ground that had to drink
The blood of child and man.

Goodbye my flowers, burnt black
By shells' awful game.
Goodbye O spirit that would not leave, the bodies
Dying young because you felt that deed forever
      wrong.
By thinking comes to mind the longings of my heart.
I walk through the houses, by shells laid bare in
      every hidden part.

Goodbye my nightbird that
Sometimes in loneliness was crying.
Goodbye O butterfly that by day
From rose to rose was flying.
Goodbye O mothers who brought up
Your children in tender care.
Goodbye fathers who always
Life's sorrow had to bear.
Goodbye O house that was my home, where I once
With my brothers and sisters was growing.
Goodbye O flowers, signs of love between friends;
They are gone when the wind of war is blowing.

THE TRUE COST OF WAR

The arms trade is the world's biggest business. More money is spent on weapons and fighting than on food production, housing and health care combined. Man, with his convoluted values, has discovered that it is more profitable to promote death than life. He prefers bullets to bread! When the end of the Cold War threatened this lucrative business in death, most arms manufacturers launched an arms push to the Third World rather than diversify into other products. However, a detailed study by the British organization Saferworld titled *The True Cost of*

Conflict, in which World Vision was an active participant, examined seven major conflicts, and provided convincing evidence that nobody ultimately benefits from war. The costs are borne by all in one form or another.

War is waste gone mad. First World War chaplain Studdert Kennedy summed it up:

> Waste of Muscle, waste of Brain,
> Waste of Patience, waste of Pain,
> Waste of Life, and waste of Health,
> Waste of Beauty, waste of Wealth,
> Waste of Blood, and waste of Tears,
> Waste of Youth's most precious Years,
> Waste of Ways the Saints have trod,
> Waste of Glory, waste of God, —
>   War![1]

The direct cost of war is the most obvious: weapons, ammunition, military operations. But what about the indirect cost? Astronomical though it is, the direct cost is only a fraction of the true cost. War in a moment of time destroys generations of patient endeavor. Public buildings, houses, factories, schools, hospitals and clinics are obliterated. Roads, bridges, railways, airfields and ports are crippled; livestock killed; tools and equipment lost.

Losses in development terms are incalculable. Vast areas of land are abandoned by displaced populations or rendered useless by land mines, with consequent loss of production and export earnings. Water supply, dams and irrigation systems are damaged. Today's internal conflicts cause a total breakdown of public services: education,

---

1. Kennedy, G. Studdert. *The Unutterable Beauty.* London: Hodder and Stoughton, 1927. p. 29.

health, transport, welfare and public administration. Resources that could be used for development go instead toward relief efforts, distorting economies and creating dependency.

The human cost is the most terrible. Until recently most casualties were soldiers. That was tragic enough; the great fields of crosses in neat rows, countless memorials listing the dead, each one representing a personal tragedy.

But in today's wars ninety per cent of the victims are civilians. They suffer mutilating injuries, brutality beyond description, massive dislocation and loss of livelihood. Small children die from starvation, exposure and loss of access to health care. More subtle, but long-lasting effects include deep psychological trauma, social fragmentation, grief, deterioration of morale and respect for life and loss of educational opportunity.

Why do we do it? I've been to practically every war zone in the world. I never get used to it. In Mozambique I've seen people come out of the bush after weeks and months trying to stay alive, eating leaves, covered with sores, a few pieces of bark clothing their emaciated bodies. In Bosnia, Fran and I sat with a family living in a pig pen in the deserted town of Vidovice. Huddled together from the cold, they told us their story. As the Serb forces advanced, most of the people fled. Two hundred decided to stay in their homes. All were slaughtered; men, women, children, babies. Every home was destroyed. Nothing was left standing. "World War II was 'mother' compared with this," said one old woman looking around at the desolation.

In Rwanda I saw the shocking sight of decapitated corpses — an estimated 100 each day — carried down the Kagera River, which forms the border with Tanzania. The same day I walked among a quarter of a million refugees in a city of plastic sheets as far as the eye could see. Long columns of refugees made their way toward the camp, carrying what they could. One woman held firmly to her one surviving child; the other three and her husband had died in Rwanda's butchery. That night I wrote a diary note by candlelight in my small tent:

As I stood among the refugees today, I felt inspired by their courage, stirred by their determination. I wanted to cry out to the world, 'Enfold these little children, stand with these anguished mothers, encourage these forlorn men with your love. Make these camps a place where a compassionate world receives them, cares for them, starts the healing work of God, restores hope.'

THE HIDDEN KILLERS

One 12-year-old Rwandan refugee, Marie, saw her father, brothers and sisters killed. She walked for two weeks to reach the camp — with one difference. Marie had only one leg. A land mine had blown off her other leg several months earlier. She had hobbled along the roads with a stick for a crutch, causing painful blisters on both hands.

The land mine has become the weapon of choice in today's warfare. It is cheap and readily available. Originally designed as an anti-tank weapon, land mines today are mainly used as a weapon of terror. They are specially-made to inflict ravaging wounds and are often laid where civilians will be the victims. In *Land Mines in Cambodia*, Physicians for Human Rights point out that, unlike bombs or artillery shells, land mines lie dormant until a person, a vehicle or an animal triggers the explosion:

They are blind weapons that cannot distinguish between the footfall of a soldier or a child at play.

They recognize no cease-fire, and long after the fighting has stopped, they can maim or kill the children and grandchildren of those who laid them.[2]

It is estimated that four million land mines lie buried in Cambodia's soil, and Battambang Province in the northwest is the worst area. Here was a challenge we felt we must take up. In 1992, World Vision joined actively in a campaign with the International Committee of Red Cross, churches and other organizations to rid the world of land mines.

It is interesting to compare World Vision's response in the 1990s with our approach when I first joined World Vision in 1968. We had a program then to provide wheelchairs and crutches for amputees. You could donate a wheelchair for $75 or a pair of crutches for $4. You could even have a plate on the wheelchair bearing your name as the donor. It was a personal and practical way of caring.

In Battambang I saw the kind of holistic, comprehensive approach that is more typical of today's World Vision. I went first to a displaced person's camp housing 20,000 people. Unable to farm because of land mines, these people were deprived of livelihood and the land's production. One day, while gathering firewood to sell, Vemok stepped on a mine, shattering his right leg, which was later amputated. He had just recovered when his wife Chaing Voen also stepped on a mine. She was eight months pregnant and lost her baby as well as her leg.

I talked with both of them in their camp shelter with their three children. They faced a crushing burden simply coping with daily life. As we take up advocacy we have to

2. Physicians for Human Rights. "Land Mines in Cambodia," Asia Watch, 1991, p. 5.

remind ourselves constantly that we are not just dealing with "issues," but with real people overwhelmed by forces beyond their control.

We dealt with land mines in six ways in Battambang:

- First, we funded the removal of mines through a British organization specializing in this dangerous work. It costs about $10 to plant a mine; over $1,000 to remove it.
- A Mines Awareness Program was conducted in every village, to help people know what to look for and what to do if they found a mine. They learned how to render first aid, how to improvise an ambulance from a bicycle, where to take the victim.
- We helped build and support an emergency clinic to treat victims. The week before my visit three had been brought in. Two were dead on arrival, the other survived after treatment.
- Counseling teams worked in the displaced people's camp to assist victims in their recovery, people like Chaing Voen and Vemok. The teams assist in getting victims to the Red Cross Centers where they receive expert medical treatment and aid in regaining mobility. Our teams help people work through their grief and shock, and begin to face the future.
- A Rehabilitation Center funded by the Australian government through World Vision provided training for suitable occupations such as motor mechanics, computer technicians, secretaries and clerical workers. This training

gave the people the dignity of self-support as an alternative to begging.

- Finally, World Vision has become one of the most active organizations working for a total ban on the manufacture, sale and use of land mines. I believe that within two years we will see land mines banned in the same way that chemical and biological weapons are banned.

I DREAM OF PEACE

"When I close my eyes, I dream of peace," said Aleksandr as he lay in a hospital bed after being severely burned by a Molotov cocktail. Aleksandr was one of 50 children whose images of war in the former Yugoslavia were published by UNICEF. How can we work together to make Aleksandr's dream come true?

First, by each one of us as a member of the human family being committed to a spirit of peace and reconciliation. I saw amazing evidence of this in a hospital right on the front line of fighting in the city of Mostar in Central Bosnia. We reached the hospital by staying close to the walls and dodging behind trees as protection against sniper fire. Even inside there was danger. That morning a patient had been hit in the knee by a bullet through the window. The medical director was Serbian, the nursing staff were Croatian and most of the patients were Moslem. These "enemies" were risking their lives to express their common humanity.

Part of the tragedy in South Africa in the apartheid era was the removal of any middle ground. Moderate voices were silenced by the government, leaving only extremes on each side. Yet the middle ground is the only place where dialogue is possible, where solutions may be found. Remove this and you are left with inevitable violence.

When F. W. De Klerk took the courageous step of removing the ban on the African National Congress and released Nelson Mandela after 27 years in prison, he took a step toward peace. Mr. Mandela, with great dignity and wisdom, resumed the walk to freedom for all South Africans. The course of history was reversed. Statements that a few months earlier would have landed a person in prison were now being made by the president. The country began to move toward what Archbishop Desmond Tutu called a "negotiated revolution." This is an infinitely preferable alternative to war, whoever might "win."

In 1993 I met the leaders of both the FRELIMO government and the RENAMO opposition in Mozambique. The prime minister said to me, "Help us hold up the flag of peace." Two days later I met Afonso Dhlakama, president of RENAMO, deep in the forest of central Mozambique. Our small plane was met at the airstrip by General Dhlakama and his aides on motorcycles. Seated on the pillion behind the general, I held on for dear life as he negotiated a rugged bush track to the clearing where we talked.

"I am now ready to cooperate," said Dhlakama during our conversation. If only there could have been cooperation 16 years earlier, before the country was destroyed and 600,000 people died! That's the kind of courage I am talking about, the courage to take initiative toward peace, to risk vulnerability as the first option, not the last.

One of the people I admire most is former Tanzanian President Julius Nyerere. I have had the privilege of two lengthy personal meetings with him. "It takes more than a flag and a national anthem to create a nation," he said. "We must learn to share power. This is true everywhere, not only in Africa."

The churches and other religious faiths have an enormous responsibility because of their influence over three quarters of the world's population, not just to talk peace, but to practice it. For this reason I issued a worldwide Call to Prayer for Peace in June 1993. But even as we pray, it gets back to individual and corporate responsibility.

In January 1991, the week the Gulf War broke out, I was in London en route to Lebanon. My flight was cancelled due to the crisis, so I went to Geneva to consult with the UN and to get an alternative flight to Beirut. Several difficult administrative matters weighed on my mind, and now despite all our prayers, war had come. I felt overwhelmed. While waiting for my flight, I wrote these verses:

PRAYER AND WAR

"Prayer changes things,"
they said.
But does it?
Half the world prayed
for peace,
but war came instead.

Perhaps it was too late
for prayer.
The seeds of war
were sown already.
Prayer was needed
before sin had its way.

I don't say,
"Prayer changes things."
I say,
"God changes hearts."
Prayer is opening the heart
to the ways of God.

Hearts that should have been open
had other agendas,
other desires, other priorities.
They missed the signals
that, if seen in time,
might have led to peace.

But why do I point to others?
How many signals
do I miss?
How many seeds of sin
do I allow to find place
in my disobedient heart?

There they grow,
fed by sloth, blindness
and every evil desire,
until they burst forth,
ugly and full grown,
to take me unaware.

So, sin has its way
with me too...
and against my will.
Will alone is not enough.
It is too weak,
too easily seduced.

Jesus alone
makes me whole.
He is the good seed
that grows and forms
the life of God
within my eager soul.

Bob Pierce's powerful documentaries awakened many American Christians to a world of need.

Ted Engstrom brought financial and management stability to a growing young Christian organization.

Gladys Aylward, whose true-life story was the basis for the film, "Inn of the Sixth Happiness," with the author, his wife Fran and daughter Jo.

The National Pediatric Hospital in Cambodia, where World Vision provided staffing and medical supplies.

Operation Seasweep" searched the South China Sea for boat people such as these, raising public awareness and transporting hundreds of refugees to safety.

In the Sri Lankan village of Heenapela, villagers are released from crushing debt.

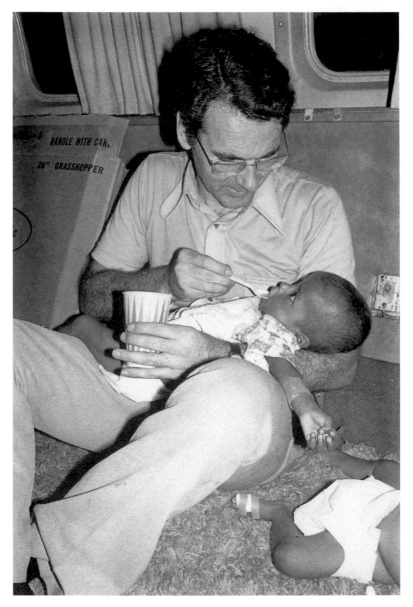

The author in-flight on the Baby Lift out of Cambodia, April 1975.

The author with members of the Korean Children's Choir.

Dr. Tony Atkins headed World Vision's therapeutic feeding program at the height of Ethiopia's crisis.

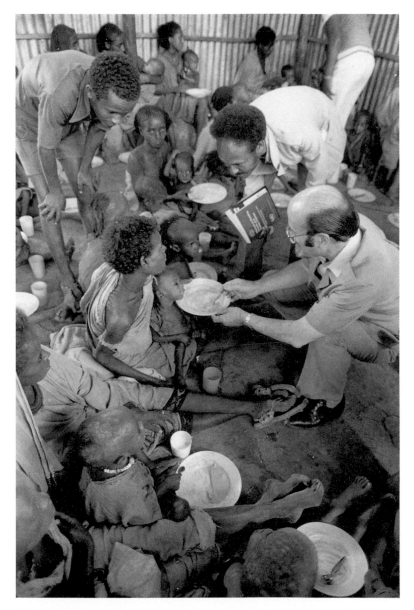

Tom Houston (right) at a feeding center in famine-struck Ethiopia in 1985.

"Agpaks" of seeds and tools in a water bucket help Mozambican deslocados (displaced people) begin their lives again.

World Vision has helped to establish Christian libraries in the former Soviet Union.

Creating sources of clean water helps people make lasting improvements in their health.

A 12-year-old land mine victim, shows the author her hand worn raw as she hobbled from Rwanda to a refugee camp in Tanzania.

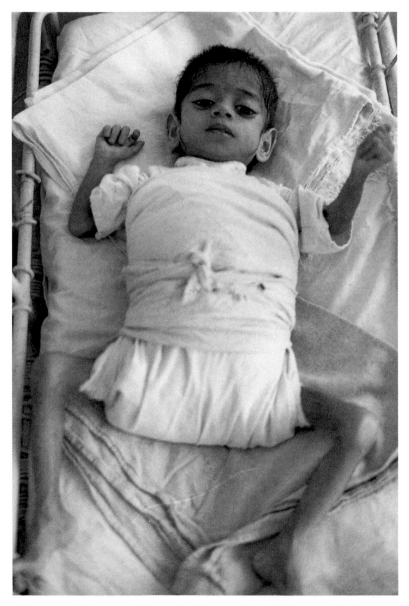

The appalling conditions for Romanian children suffering from AIDS led World Vision in 1991 to develop educational programs for frightened caregivers and parents.

Dr. Sam Kamaleson in Poland with Metropolitan Bazyli Doroszkiewicz of the Orthodox Church.

On a 1976 Australian "This Is Your Life" television program, the author is encircled by: (clockwise from left) his mother, daughter Jo, Oh Mee Soon, daughter Ros, and wife Fran.

Part V

A Journey Together

World Vision is about being the hands, feet and arms of Jesus.

— Virginia Woodward, World Vision Jerusalem

12

Sharing Faith

"Why should World Vision be involved in sanitation, hygiene or agriculture?" asked a member of the India Board. "Are we becoming a secular agency? Is our job to change structures or to change hearts?"

The occasion was a strategic planning meeting of the India Board and senior staff in 1979. Fifteen years later a member of the International Board asked, "Are we evangelical or ecumenical?"

These are inevitable questions as the scope of World Vision's ministry becomes more comprehensive and the range of church relationships broadens. Former, well-defined boundaries seem to be unclear. One support office board member put it more bluntly. "We have lost our moorings," he said.

I want to look at our mission from several angles in this chapter. To change metaphors, it is like holding a prism up to a ray of light. As the ray passes through the prism, the light emerges in different colors, but all are expressions of the same light. So in World Vision, we see the various aspects of our mission, not as being apart from the light of Christ, nor as camouflaged methods of exposing people to the light, as if we were setting some kind of religious booby-trap, but as different manifestations of the light given to the world in Jesus Christ. Though I have called this chapter "Sharing Faith," every chapter of the book expresses a dimension of the gospel of Jesus Christ.

FOLLOWING JESUS

Let us start, not with tradition but with Jesus, as our Mission Statement reminds us to do. What do we learn from him about the scope of mission and relationships?

Jesus announced his own mission in the words of the prophet Isaiah, "The Spirit of the Lord is upon me, because he has anointed me to preach good news to the poor. He has sent me to proclaim freedom for the prisoners and recovery of sight for the blind, to release the oppressed, to proclaim the year of the Lord's favor."

To an astonished audience in the synagogue at Nazareth he said, "Today this scripture is fulfilled in your hearing." At first the crowd marvelled at the grace of Jesus' words. Then they became offended. "Isn't this Joseph's son?"

Seeing this limited, restrictive view of God's love, Jesus gave two examples of the expansive mercy of God — the healing of Naaman the Syrian, and the provision of famine relief to a widow in Sidon, neither of them Jewish. This was too much! Jesus was roughly handled and threatened with violent death.

But some people did hear Jesus' message. His invitation, "Come to me, all you who labor and are burdened;" brought a stream of the lame, the deformed, the rejected, all longing to be healed.

Meanwhile, John the Baptist, who had first announced Jesus as the long-awaited Messiah, had been imprisoned. Matthew, in Chapter 11, tells us, "When John heard in prison what Christ was doing, he sent his disciples to ask him, 'Are you the one who was to come, or should we look for another?'" The inference is that John didn't like what he heard.

In reply, Jesus reaffirmed the theme of the Nazareth announcement. "Go back and tell John what you hear and see: The blind receive sight, the lame walk, those who have leprosy are cured, the deaf hear, the dead are raised and the good news is preached to the poor." And for added emphasis, Jesus issued a mild rebuke, "Blessed is the person who does not fall away on account of me."

Why should John doubt? Perhaps the discouragement of prison; or because Jesus' personality and message were so different from his own. Maybe it was a matter of timing — John thought that Jesus, the Messiah, would bring deliverance faster. Whatever the reason, he had different expectations, which seem connected to "what Jesus was doing."

Human beings at heart are analysts. We like to take things apart, understand how they work. But we get into trouble when we try to fragment the gospel of Jesus Christ. Jesus put no one aspect of his ministry above another. There is no hierarchy of activities or values. We cannot conclude from his words or actions that preaching is more important than healing, or that God is more present in the sanctuary than in the street.

Instead we see a beautiful wholeness about his approach to ministry. This is where we get our word holistic (Greek holos, whole), being concerned with wholes or with complete systems rather than with the analysis of, treatment of, or dissection into, parts. World Vision's Declaration of Internationalization of 1978, referring to "countless millions of human beings caught in the toils of poverty, hunger, disease, loneliness and despair," went on:

Our approach to this staggering need is holistic: we decline the unBiblical concept of the spiritual over against the physical, the personal over against the social. It is the whole person in the wholeness of his or her relationships that we want to see redeemed through the one Savior, Jesus Christ our Lord.

A Question Of Percentages

How much is spent on evangelism? This is a frequent question, from both friends and critics. To some, what we spend is not enough. To others, it should be nothing at all. I was once pressed hard for a specific percentage of time and money dedicated to evangelism. I turned to the gospel of John, Chapter 9, for my reply.

Seeing a blind beggar on the streets of Jerusalem, the disciples asked Jesus, "Who sinned, this man or his parents, that he should be born blind?"

"Neither," replied Jesus, "But that the work of God might be seen."

Jesus proceeded then to restore the man's sight. Rejoicing, the man told everyone. The religious authorities were not interested in the miracle of healing, but only in the name and whereabouts of someone who dared to do this on the Sabbath. When the man defended Jesus, they cursed his insolence and threw him out. It did not occur to them that they could learn anything from a blind beggar! When Jesus heard that they had thrown him out, he found the man. "Do you believe in the Son of Man?" asked Jesus.

"Who is he, sir?" replied the man. "Tell me so that I may believe in him."

"You have now seen him," said Jesus. "In fact, he is the one speaking with you."

"Lord, I believe," declared the man, and he worshiped him.

My question then was, "What percentage of Jesus' time was devoted to healing, what to restoring the man's dignity by searching him out and what percentage to bringing him to faith?"

I regard the question as irrelevant. The real question is, in situations of suffering, poverty, injustice and evil are God's servants there? Are they reflecting the fullness of God's character in who they are, in what they do, in what they say? Do they respond with the tender, compassionate, insightful love of God that we see in this story. In our blindness we Christians too often insist on a stereotyped approach to faith and witness, an approach that employs certain words or methods, certain theological propositions. I do not see that in Jesus.

Holism is not merely a collection of activities and certainly it is not handing out tracts or Bibles with food. A holistic approach to faith is an attitude of mind, a way of thinking about life and creation, a sense of the presence of God in every situation, a regard for the dignity and worth of people. It is what we see in the person and ministry of Jesus Christ.

Serving The Church

World Vision's Mission Statement includes a commitment to "Strategic Initiatives that serve the Church in the fulfillment of its mission."

One of these initiatives is the pastors' conference ministry originally under the leadership of Dr. Paul Rees and, since 1974, of Dr. Samuel Kamaleson. Since the first conference in Korea in 1953, World Vision has sponsored nearly 250 conferences in 59 countries on all continents. Over 110,000 men and women have attended: pastors and priests, youth leaders, seminary students, church leaders, Christian workers and missionaries in various fields.

The conferences are not promoted as a World Vision project. They result from needs felt within the Christian community in any country leading to an invitation to World Vision. A process of mutual planning follows in which the national organizing committee, representing the widest possible range of churches, works with World Vision to decide conference themes, speakers, budget and other planning aspects. The costs are always shared by the participants and World Vision. The conferences usually run for five days and include public meetings in the evenings. In recent years, spouses of the pastors and women in ministry have been included as participants.

The ecumenical environment of the conferences reinforces the unity of the church and widens the area of fellowship, while the challenge of scripture deepens commitment. Nowhere has this been more evident than in Eastern Europe, where the church withstood 70 years of persecution and now faces a difficult period of readjustment, including more open contact with churches of the West. In many countries Christians hastened the new day, like those in Timisoara, Romania, who defied the tyrant Ceaucescu.

UNDER SUSPICION!

World Vision had worked quietly in Romania during the most difficult years and one month before Ceaucescu's downfall, World Vision's vice president-at-large, Dr. Sam Kamaleson, was in Bucharest for a Christian leadership conference. He had been followed everywhere by the secret police and was due to speak at a large youth rally on the Saturday night. The morning of the rally, Sam and Charles Rogers, who had succeeded Ralph Hamburger as East Europe director, were called to a meeting with two agents of the Securitate, the Romanian secret police.

Chuck Rogers takes up the story:

We found ourselves sitting across a table from two very sinister-looking characters who let us know, in no uncertain terms, that they were aware of our activities, that they did not approve, and that we were not welcome in Romania.

They went on to tell Sam that his preaching must stop. Knowing that the church would be packed with eager young people that night, I wondered how Sam would respond. After a slight pause he turned to the chief interrogator and said, "If I can't preach, may I sing?" For the first time a smile came across the faces of the two agents.

"Sing? Of course you can sing. You can sing till your throat hurts!"

That night the auditorium was packed with young people. When it was time for the sermon, Sam stood in the pulpit, looked out on the audience, and said, "I've been told not to preach tonight, so instead I would like to sing to you." But Sam found it necessary to follow each song, and sometimes each verse, with some commentary. So that night he sang in his rich baritone, he spoke, he sang, he spoke; and at the end of the service there was a powerful outpouring of God's Spirit.

I believe that, thanks to the secret police, more was accomplished for the Kingdom of God than if they had left us alone!

Pastors' conferences at critical times in countries like Ethiopia and Cambodia have either helped prepare the church for coming trials, or encouraged Christians at a time of renewal and opportunity.

Other doors constantly open for Sam Kamaleson to engage in strategic outreach. Recently he spoke to leading business executives in Malaysia on the theme, How do I live the gospel? As part of World Vision's agreement with Sam when he joined the team 20 years ago, he spends a portion of each year in his home country, India. In 1995 he gave several addresses to 200,000 people attending the 100th convention of the historic Mar Thoma Church in South India. He is the servant-leader of several strategic ministries within India, completely staffed and supported by Indians.

MARC And Unreached People

In the years following World War II traditional missions encountered a time of ferment. Independence movements were sweeping the world and many missions were seen to be associated with the colonial past. At the same time new specialized agencies were emerging on the evangelical scene like Mission Aviation Fellowship, Wycliffe Bible Translators, Youth for Christ and World Vision itself. This climate of ferment and change suited innovative thinkers like Ed Dayton, an American aerospace engineer, who was intrigued by the possibility of harnessing the tools of technology and management to the task of world mission.

While studying theology at Fuller Seminary in Pasadena, Ed pioneered a concept he called MARC, Missions Advanced Research and Communications Center, with World Vision support. MARC became a division of World Vision in 1967, thus starting a distinctive contribution to mission thinking and practice. Ed's main goal was to change the way people thought about mission.

"Are you familiar with the systems approach to problems?" was Ed's first question to me when I met him soon after I joined World Vision in 1968. "Well...er...not exactly!" was something like my reply. Ed proceeded to change my thinking, or at least to expand it.

"It's good to have fellowship," Ed would say, "but it's even better to have fellowship around the facts." MARC set out to assemble information on world mission through careful research, sharing the findings with all who wished to receive its publications. Planning Strategies for World Evangelization became a major book from MARC and the theme of many seminars.

The Unreached Peoples concept promoted by MARC helped churches and Christian workers to think about people in distinctive cultural groups, which in turn shaped the most appropriate means of communicating the good news of Jesus Christ. The MARC team also gave extended and formative support to other strategic Christian movements such as the Lausanne Committee for World Evangelization, urban ministry initiatives and consultations on Islam and Christianity.

Initially MARC operated like a subsidiary of World Vision with its own identity and networks, its special constituency and funding base. In the late 1970s we began to shift the focus of MARC's research and learnings more toward World Vision's programs of relief and development. Today's MARC, led by Bryant Myers, vice president for Holistic Ministry Resources, has a high level of integration with our total ministry.

The story of MARC illustrates the capacity of World Vision to take strategic initiatives, often acting as a catalyst for releasing other resources and ideas, in serving the larger vision of the Kingdom of God.

WORKING WITH OR THROUGH THE CHURCH

In earlier times, it seemed natural for World Vision to form a relationship with a local church to work in a community. We spoke of working "through the church." In many cases this created a dangerous situation. If the local church actually became the project partner, responsible for the project, this put the church in the position of a "power broker," dispensing benefits to the community. The risk of the church using these "benefits" to put pressure on people to join the church or become Christians was almost inevitable. This approach also could have a divisive effect among churches if there were more than one church in the community. Sometimes the pastor would personally assume control of the project, increasing the possibility of World Vision becoming a corrupting influence.

We discovered that a far better way was to ask the community to elect a committee or "core group," with accountability to the community. This placed ownership for the project with the community itself, a key factor in the development process. In the initial dialogue with the community at the formative stage of a project relationship, the Christian identity and mission of World Vision was made clear. We also emphasized that the project was for the whole community, not just for Christians. This method allowed Christians of all the churches to be "yeast" or "light" or "salt" in the manner described by Jesus. It also enabled World Vision to be a unifying influence among churches rather than a divisive one. This approach is what I mean by working "with" the church rather than "through" the church.

HEARING AND ENCOURAGING THE CHURCH

At the height of the Ethiopia famine, Russ Kerr (now World Vision's vice president for relief), Tony Atkins and Ethiopia Director Solomon Lulu met with respected leaders of three churches — Kale Heywat, Mekane Yesus and Ethiopian Orthodox.

The country was in the grip not only of the drought but also of the repressive Mengistu regime. The conclusions reached in this crucial meeting were:

If the World Vision response to the famine was to have any lasting impact we needed to recognize that:

- there is a body of believers in Ethiopia who remain faithful despite great persecution.
- it will ultimately be through the endurance of a suffering church that the people will find peace and be fed.
- we anticipate an indeterminate period of further persecution for the church.
- we should expect no softening in the position of the government out of gratitude for aid received.
- the priorities of the government are, first, the maintenance of total control, second, ideological

purity and third, the industrialization of the
nation.
- the welfare of its citizens does not figure at all in
the priorities of the government.
- house churches will continue to be the main or
only means of fellowship for almost all
Ethiopian Christians.
- God will be revealed by how Christians
worldwide respond to the famine and then in the
response of Ethiopian Christians to the need of
their country for peace and integrity in national
life.
- it may be the very character of the World Vision
emergency response that enables the faithful
persistence of the church.
- consistent with this view World Vision needs a
long term commitment to Ethiopia.

These principles became a key reference point in
planning the enormous relief effort that followed.

OPENING DOORS OF OPPORTUNITY

Because of the flexibility of World Vision's different
streams of ministry, it is possible to be a partner with the
church in difficult environments, while truly serving the
needs of people. Following the May 1991 downfall of the
Mengistu regime in Ethiopia we knew that there were
serious needs in the province of Tigray, which had been
inaccessible during the war. When the Tigrean People's
Liberation Force took control of the country, I decided to
visit Tigray for a field assessment in July of 1991. However,
we could not get permission.

Finally, with our Ethiopia team, I met with the
government person responsible. He was a tough, young

freedom fighter, just in from the bush. There was no protocol, no handshake, no smile, just a brooding feeling of hostility as we entered his room.

"Well, why should I let World Vision go to Tigray?" he began.

I gave a brief background of World Vision, feeling defensive about our cool reception. My veteran colleague, Ato Tsega Mariam, former Ethiopia director and now East Africa regional director, saved the day. Quietly he explained how World Vision sits down with the people in a community, hears their story, works out ideas together for improving their life. He described how this help was not dependent on religion, but was available to all. We invited churches to cooperate with us in this effort as part of the community, he said. Our official started to relax and listen.

Then one of those amazing things happened that I regard as the action of God. A colleague of the official had just returned from London and was in the meeting with us. In London he had attended a meeting where he met Jeff Thindwa, our former director in Malawi and now a member of the World Vision U.K. executive team. Jeff impressed him. Taking the official aside, he told him, "This is a good organization." The decision was made; permission was granted.

We flew to Tigray two days later and drove deep into the mountains over rugged, washed-out roads. Severe need was evident everywhere and the groundwork was laid out for a relief program, leading on to development. We did not engage in preaching, but were able to bring encouragement and support to the people and open a door of opportunity for the church.

We have learned that World Vision does not have to "do it all." To insist that we do is one of the most subtle forms of a lack of faith in God. In most places we are able to express our mission fully. In other places we cannot. Taking a holistic approach does not mean that in every situation there must be a direct sharing of faith. We may be the vital forerunner for others. They will come later and build on what we have done. Remember the words of St. Paul, "I planted the seed, Apollos watered it, but God made it grow" (1 Cor. 3:6).

ONE CHURCH, ONE FAITH, ONE LORD

Personally, I have worked consistently over the whole of my 28 years with World Vision to broaden our relationships with the church at every level. The process has been infinitely enriching to me as I have discovered new frontiers of fellowship. I also believe it has enhanced the stature of World Vision.

While based in Geneva, I enjoyed sharing in the Monday morning worship services at the World Council of Churches, conducted in its beautiful chapel and rich in the diversity of liturgy and multi-cultural expressions of faith. Or high in the mountains of Irian Jaya, I have worshiped with Dani tribespeople in utter simplicity of faith in Jesus Christ, sheltered from the scorching sun by a huge thatched meeting house, open at the sides for ventilation. Worlds apart culturally, but one in Jesus Christ.

I have sought the privilege of meeting with leaders of the churches in the many countries I have visited — Roman Catholic, Orthodox, Protestant. Without exception these conversations have yielded new insights, fresh understanding and deeper knowledge of each other. Often they have built new trust.

On one occasion I went to Germany for meetings with church leaders who had been critical of World Vision.

I did not know what to expect, for I knew we had provoked the criticism to some extent by our own actions. What kind of hostility would I encounter? In every case I was received courteously and warmly.

One meeting was with our most severe critic. Instead of the formidable adversary I expected, I found a compassionate, gentle Christian brother. He bore the marks of suffering from a personal disability and reflected the depth of character that suffering often produces. His parting words as I left were, "You are welcome at any time." We had been able to hear each other. As Henri Nouwen once put it, "The Christ in you met with the Christ in me."

Lebanon is one of the best examples of ecumenical relationships in World Vision. Director Jean Bouchebl is a model for all of us in prayer, personal witness and faith. At the same time, he has built relationships with all churches. Their leaders at the most senior levels know him and trust him, while in the project communities he has developed working relationships with all denominations. Archbishop Aram Keshishian, Armenian Catholicos of Cilicia and moderator of the Central Committee of the World Council of Churches, expressed to me the hope that this could be a model for the whole of World Vision. I agreed.

There are those who would like to write World Vision's agenda for us, based on theological issues or traditional relationships. In one country some conservative Christians refused to attend a meeting because we had invited a Roman Catholic sister with whom we had project work. They interpreted our inclusiveness as a sign that we were abandoning old friends. They could not see that you do not have to agree on everything or deny your own convictions to have fellowship with another.

And what are our convictions in World Vision? The clearest answer is given in the policy on Christian witness developed carefully by a special commission out of our experience and theological reflection. The policy was adopted by the International Board in March 1995:

In a world of increasing pain, suffering, injustice, conflict and alienation from the God who created it, World Vision understands Christian witness as testifying to the revelation of God in Jesus Christ, who offers his redemption to all, and announcing Christ's lordship over the whole of creation — persons, communities, structures and nature. We testify of God by who we are and what we do and say, and by pointing to his signs and miracles. Being witnesses of Christ is foundational to our understanding of holistic ministry and is the integrating principle for all aspects of our mission: transformational development, emergency relief, promotion of justice, strategic initiatives and public awareness. The phrase, "that encourages people to respond to the gospel," means it is our sincere hope that people will repent and come to personal faith in Jesus Christ.

The policy goes on to elaborate how this witness is made effective by who we are and what we do.

This is where we have come in our way of sharing faith. Others may have different ways, for there is no one right way to make known this good news. I sometimes think we try to be wiser than Jesus himself when we profess to have all the answers.

I understand the concerns of those who may feel we are drifting from our moorings. For my part, I do not want to sail on a boat that is held fast to a mooring. I want to feel the exhilaration of the voyage, the wind filling the sails, the spray in my face. Yes, there is a risk of getting off course. But Jesus has given us a pilot in the Holy Spirit and a chart in the Holy scriptures. I will trust them to bring us safely home.

This brings us back to the question, "Are we evangelical or ecumenical?" It is my belief that we must be both and it saddens me that the two are so often stated as if they are contrary positions. Jesus said, "By this will all the world know that you are my disciples, that you love one another."

In the last hours of his life on earth, Jesus prayed passionately that those who followed him "may all be one, as you and I are one, that the world may believe that you have sent me" (John 17:21). Jesus left no doubt that a spirit of unity is the most powerful factor in sharing faith. More than that, he called it a "new commandment." "I give you a new commandment," he said, "that you love one another as I have loved you" (John 13:34). Unity is not merely a desirable option, it is the command of Christ.

Perhaps part of the problem is that we have tried to institutionalize unity in structures like the World Council of Churches and National Councils of Churches, just as we tend to institutionalize evangelicalism in bodies like the World Evangelical Fellowship and National Evangelical Association. These structures develop a life of their own and may polarize rather than unify the community of faith.

I believe all Christians need to recapture the simplicity of Christ's words to us; to share our faith in him so that others may also believe and pass from death to life, as he said they would; and to extend the area of fellowship rather than narrow it. If we fail to do this, we make the Body of Christ into what Thomas Merton called "a body of broken bones."

A church at war within itself and with no message of life has nothing to offer a broken world. Evangelical and ecumenical — that's what the world needs.

Having identified Isaiah 65:17-25 as the organization's vision for poor communities, this became a unifying factor that rallied the whole organization. The vision focuses on transformation of relationships — with God, with self, with people and with environment. Pursuing this vision made us conscious of the need to seek the same transformation for the organization and for individual staff.

— Evita Perez, World Vision Philippines

Are Organizations Hopeless?

"What's the point of all this stuff?" I exclaimed in exasperation, as I swept the papers off my table to the floor. Then, turning to a heap of reports and documents behind me, I dumped them into the waste paper basket as well.

"It's all useless clutter!" I muttered.

My colleague, Peter Berry, director of communications, did not say a word. He quietly picked up the papers from the floor and put them back on my round table. He understood my frustration with institutional machinery. He felt it too — and who has not? I never did take the documents out of the waste paper basket and, as far as I know, their loss made no difference to anything!

My favorite "good news, bad news" story was told to me by Frank Edwards of the Louis Allen organization. "The good news is that World Vision is cutting through the red tape. The bad news is that they are cutting it lengthwise!"

Big organizations can get in their own way, falling over themselves, tangled up in their own systems. They become self-serving rather than being instruments to serve others. Almost without realizing it leaders find that they are in a prison of their own making. The organizations they create can hinder rather than help achieve the mission.

Organizing For Ministry

People often ask me, "How does a big organization like World Vision balance Christian values with the practice of management?" My honest and personal answer is, "With considerable difficulty."

As in many other aspects of life, the values that emerge from Jesus' life and teaching seem at odds with organizational behavior and politics. This is not to say that integration is impossible, but that it cannot be taken for granted. I have used the following principles to help move World Vision toward the kind of organizational character I regard as Christian:

1. The organization is servant, not master. Ideally, caring is a person-to-person relationship. In the modern world, this relationship is largely mediated through organizations, especially if the caring ministry extends beyond local boundaries. As the organization gets larger it tends to become impersonal and bureaucratic. As one writer said, "Bureaucracy is a means of carrying out transactions between strangers." The organization takes on a life of its own, absorbing the energy of its people like a huge machine. Instead of serving its purpose, or better still, serving other people, the organization serves itself. For the Christian, Paul offers a different perspective in 2

Corinthians 4:6, "We don't proclaim ourselves, but Jesus Christ as Lord, and ourselves your servants for Jesus' sake."

2. The leader does not have to do it all. One of the subtle traps of leadership is the belief, conscious or not, that the leader has to be the only source of inspiration and ideas — the all-wise, all-knowing, all-powerful executive or visionary — ahead of everyone else, better than everyone else, always at center stage. That is not to say the leader does not lead, like the person who said, "I must follow that crowd — I'm their leader!" But the best leaders will always open themselves to wisdom other than their own, wisdom from both within and outside the organization. Being on a journey together means listening to one's companions on the way.

We are accustomed to talking about a "firm hand on the tiller." But, except in times of emergency, the best sailors use a light hand on the tiller so they can feel the movement of their boat. They look ahead to see the "wind shifts" that indicate a more favorable course. They listen to their crew and benefit from combined experience. They read all these signals and are ready to "go about" quickly and confidently at the right time.

Latin America vice president, Manfred Grellert, told me that it took two years of listening and basic participation to get a sense of definition and direction for the ministry of World Vision in Latin America, before the mature understanding and strategic organization of today began to take shape.

3. Shared leadership replaces the organizational pyramid. Pyramids were invented by the Egyptians to bury their dead. Rigid adherence to the organizational pyramid may be suitable for dead organizations, but not for the living. After a conversation with a young pastor in El

Salvador a few years ago, he said to me, "I often wondered what the thinking was at the top of the World Vision pyramid. It's hard to know at the bottom."

"That's why it's good to flatten out the pyramid," I replied.

The organization of the future will move farther and farther away from the traditional pyramid with its hierarchy of authority. That is why I have encouraged a concept of shared leadership over the years.

Shared leadership does not mean that everyone tries to do everybody else's job. Work is carefully defined and assigned. But shared leadership recognizes individual strengths and weaknesses in every person, and that the whole is greater than the sum of its parts. Through a participative team approach, the strengths of one benefit all and the weaknesses of one are borne by all.

Shared leadership requires a spirit of unity; a high level of cooperation rather than competition. It involves a sense of mutual responsibility for the whole enterprise as well as one's own particular part in it. It is specially suited to large organizations with widely-dispersed, interdependent national entities, like World Vision.

Building an understanding of this approach takes time, and risk. Middle managers feel deprived of power, senior managers feel threatened, those traditionally at the bottom of the heap can also feel insecure when the old boundaries fall away. But just as we have learned to risk trusting people in the development process, so also must we apply the same principles in the organization that would support human development.

Part of the problem, especially in Christian organizations, is that we have a stereotyped view of leadership. We tend to view leadership as a type of personality or a special set of skills. There is no question that personality and skill play their part. But I have always regarded leadership as a combination of factors, the right person to do a certain job at a particular time. The kind of leader needed in one situation and time may be quite different from the leader needed for another. This is why it is not helpful to make comparisons between leaders.

4. Becoming a Learning Organization. Joan Levett was a vice president of World Vision International for just over two years before she passed away in March 1995. Her death deprived us of her keen mind and disciplined work. Part of her job was to help World Vision become a learning organization. As Joan put it, this means:

It is an organization where people learn together.

It is one where there is team learning and leadership; an organization that focuses on people and process rather than only product; creating synergy, where one plus one equals more than two.

An organization that sees things whole, where there is connectedness and integration rather than fragmentation in individual parts. An organization that is dynamic, not static; with courage to take risks, experiment, face change. Also to be vulnerable, able to admit mistakes and failure; to try again and do it better next time.

It is an organization where learnings come out of practice and are applied, through a constant process of action, reflection, action. An organization that is strategic; proactive rather than reactive, and where decisions are made within the framework of overall strategy. One which is not afraid of diversity and the creative tension it generates.

An organization that listens; where people are valued above systems and procedures; which has vision shared by all and not just top management; where both participation and leadership go hand in hand.

Joan and I agreed that World Vision is not yet that kind of organization, but that we aspire to it and work seriously toward it. To that I need to add that World Vision may well be that kind of organization in some places, for I have already argued against the kind of monolithic uniformity that is imposed from the center!

5. *Learning from failure.* "Where did you learn all these things?" I once asked a colleague whose brilliant work in a project community had become a model for the whole country.

"From all the mistakes I made in the last project," he replied.

One of our most disappointing failures was NewsVision, our London-based news service. NewsVision was a bold, imaginative concept. It was to be a small, specialized news service offering fast, accurate news coverage to the media on events and issues affecting the poor among whom we work. A form of advocacy, really. The idea was to build credibility with the media for the quality and depth of our material, using World Vision's global network of contacts.

Impending disaster was the focus. Our plan was to get an early warning about the disaster and be ready to make an appeal for funds to coincide with media reports. If we could actually break the news to the media, so much the better. We recruited the former managing editor of one of the world's largest television news services as editor-in-chief. We were set to go!

Our approach was to build relationships with key international media people, establish a 24-hour contact service, help arrange visits to disaster areas by strategically-placed journalists and TV units, provide resource material to the media and develop our internal communications network to support the plan.

The concept of NewsVision came from a meeting of World Vision communicators from several countries in 1987. I was asked by Tom Houston to take the idea and get it off the ground from my office in Geneva. Unfortunately, the call to return to Monrovia as acting president came just as NewsVision was about to be launched. I was unable to give it the personal attention that later events showed it badly needed.

After four years the International Board decided to close NewsVision due to cost and management problems. It was a sad day for me; a good idea gone sour. Some very good work had been done and I believe we got our money's worth from NewsVision. But I recognized the problems and felt personally responsible. I had not ensured that an adequate foundation was laid in the beginning. If the foundation is not right, the building will not stand.

Yet I am glad we attempted NewsVision. Not everything is going to work the way you want. There will inevitably be failure, but that should not stop us taking the risk of doing the new and different.

6. Do not expect perfection. "Many trifles make perfection," goes an old saying, "but perfection is no trifle." Indeed it is not — nor is it attainable in the work of human transformation or the organizational arrangements needed to support it.

Expectations can be unrealistic, especially in Christian organizations. We forget that Jesus did not always succeed in his encounter with humanity. Not everyone who met Jesus became a believer. The rich young ruler went away "sorrowful." Even those who did believe often fell short. Some fell away. One of Jesus' closest companions betrayed him.

Somehow we seem to expect perfection of ourselves and of others, and are disappointed or disillusioned when it does not happen. We need to aim high, but be willing to accept less than perfection as a worthy result.

How Much Reaches The Poor?

This is the most frequently asked question about World Vision, and indeed any aid organization. And it is a fair question. However, it is not the most important question. The real question is, "How are the lives of people changed for the better because of my help?" That is the result donors want to see. That is why they give and I believe that is where we should start the discussion.

In Chapter Five I gave some examples of how change takes place in poor communities. You will recall that bringing about change requires more than money, especially if the results are to last. That is what is meant by "sustainable development" —enabling the people to reach a point where they can continue the development process without outside help. Achieving that result requires women and men skilled in community organization to come alongside the community, encourage them to believe in the possibility of change and to work together to improve their conditions of life. Our investment in these development workers (usually grouped in "area teams") is the most valuable contribution we can make to alleviating poverty. As Philip Hunt of World Vision Australia puts it, we are a "transform" rather than a "transfer" organization.

Having said that, we still come back to the question of the cost of running the organization. What is necessary to do good and reliable work? How much is too much? What does it take to get the attention of a public bombarded with messages? How can we make the most of opportunities for ministry within acceptable limits of risk and prudence? What is an appropriate organizational "life-style?" These are not easy judgment calls.

The first international meeting I attended for World Vision took place in Singapore in 1968. When I arrived at the appointed hotel I decided it was too expensive. So I moved next door to one that had been suggested to me as more in keeping with our work among the poor. I found myself in a dormitory with twelve other men. The facilities were minimal, communication was impossible and the safety of the food and dormitory questionable. Meanwhile, I discovered that I was to have shared a room in the original hotel with World Vision's director in Korea, Marlin Nelson, one of our distinguished pioneers. After the first night I moved back and joined Marlin!

The issue here is not whether one is willing to accept the conditions of the dormitory. I have slept in dormitories, in tents, on airport floors and in the open air all over the world! In those cases it was a matter of necessity and I just did it. But where there is a choice it is a question of deciding a level that allows you to function efficiently without extravagance. Usually it is somewhere between the two examples I have described in Singapore.

A good reference point is to keep in mind who owns the resources. The funds do not belong to the organization, but to the poor. Therefore, all who work in the organization are trustees of those resources, and need to use them wisely and carefully to accomplish the purpose for which they have been given. Personally I have found it important to stay in touch as far as possible with the conditions under which the very poor have to live; to go to where they are, sit with them in their dwellings, sometimes in utter wretchedness, hear their stories, feel and smell the atmosphere of their existence.

Even as I write these words, there comes to my mind the picture of a small boy I encountered in a huge settlement of displaced people in Mozambique. His thin body was clothed in a few tattered rags. Breaking off from the group, I went over and sat on the ground beside him. His name was Frederico. I asked him how he was feeling. Putting his hand to his chest, he replied, "My heart hurts."

As I talked with Frederico, a little procession passed bearing a small bundle wrapped in hessian — another victim of war's merciless impact on children.

Later, I met a group of children in a refugee school. When I knelt to greet a tiny girl, she gathered the few shreds of her once-green frock around her. I looked at the one hundred or so other children. Not one of them had adequate clothing and cold weather was approaching.

That same day I learned of a plane trip that had been arranged for a staff interview. A colleague who was with me pointed out that the plane fare would clothe Frederico and all the children in the school we had just visited. Accordingly the trip was cancelled and the interview handled another way. And one hundred excited children received warm and colorful clothing!

The action was symbolic too. I shared the experience with the whole of World Vision as a reminder that we are accountable to the poor as well as to donors. My purpose was not to create guilt. Journeys have to be made, necessary equipment must be purchased, salaries have been earned and need to be paid. But these decisions are to be made as a conscious act of stewardship. "Think twice and spend once," I said to our staff.

WHAT ABOUT SPONSORSHIP?

"We have serious concerns about the sponsorship of children," said a German church leader with whom I was meeting. As we talked, the same criticisms came out that I have heard many times in many places over the years. Sponsorship is seen as an expensive, sentimental and paternalistic response to the needs of children. Some feel it singles out certain children from others for special treatment. Many believe it is anti-developmental. Some even regard it as a form of exploitation of children.

Sponsorship is attractive to donors. The program links a particular child with a donor (sponsor), who contributes a monthly amount to assist in the child's care and development.

The sponsor receives a photo of the child and may exchange correspondence.

Like other aspects of World Vision's work, sponsorship has undergone tremendous changes based on our experience in working with children. Starting with the institutional care of orphaned and handicapped children after the Korean War, the program has evolved to a thoroughly developmental approach today. The developmental approach recognizes that the family and community in which the child lives has the primary responsibility for the child's well-being. Our task is to help empower the community to bring about changes in the conditions that perpetuate poverty.

At the same time we need to keep in mind that each child is a person of infinite worth. Each is uniquely individual, as all people are. Some children still need special help, perhaps institutional care. The sponsorship program recognizes this personal dimension and helps prevent children being lost in a general scheme of development or an impersonal system of aid.

In my meeting with the German church leader, I took from my wallet the photograph of Jane Namawawu, whose story I told in Chapter 10. I explained how I had met her in a village in Uganda where her family had been almost wiped out by AIDS. I described how we were working with the World Bank, the Ugandan government and the local communities in a massive program of AIDS education and support for children orphaned as a result of the disease. I gave examples of how the survivors, many of them widows, were working together to ensure that children were not left helpless and alone. I went on to tell of my meeting with the president of the World Bank, with whom I shared Jane's story by way of advocacy and encouragement.

Yet Jane was also a real person, not merely a symbol or a statistic. I had a letter from her in my pocket. My wife and I have a personal, if distant, sense of relationship with her and her sister. My story is not much different from that of over a million other sponsors, few of whom have the privilege of meeting the child they sponsor, but who care about them, pray for them, express genuine love for them.

Of course, it is easy to romanticize sponsorship and to have unrealistic expectations of what can be accomplished. We are engaged in a constant process of sponsor education to help sponsors understand the reality of the child's situation and the limitations of the program. And yes, there are additional costs in maintaining a system of correspondence, photographs and individual tracking of each child's progress. Yes, the program can be paternalistic (or maternalistic!). Yes, it can manipulate the special appeal of children for the purpose of fund-raising. All these dangers are present. But there are dangers and risks in any form of international aid if attempted without care and integrity.

We have had enough disappointments and failures in our efforts toward human transformation to keep us from being naive. We have also seen more than enough beautiful outcomes to fill us with hope and sustain our endeavors. For example, many sponsor groups in New Zealand have actually engaged in dialogue by correspondence with project communities about problems experienced in the project. Sponsorship has enabled these people on opposite sides of the world to enter into each other's lives, share their hopes and struggles. In Taiwan the sponsor of the largest number of children is herself a former sponsored child. World Vision's national director in Indonesia graduated from the sponsorship program.

In this world of shrinking distance and global awareness there is a sense in which all the children of the world belong to all the people of the world. Sponsorship helps bring this idea to life.

TRUSTEES AS PARTNERS

When we were organizing the Board of Directors for World Vision of Australia, I invited Geoff Fletcher to join. He had played a part behind the scenes in the decision to bring World Vision to Australia. He had also been a mission executive and was wary of committees. He raised an interesting question.

"Is World Vision an executive-directed, board-advised organization, or a board-controlled, executive-managed one?" Geoff asked me.

I replied that it was more the former. That was the way we operated in 1968. Some of my staff colleagues would probably like it to be that way now, or dispense with boards completely.

My view is that neither alternative states the ideal position. The trustee or board role is vital to a healthy, non-profit organization, quite apart from the fact that a board is usually required by law. I have seen too much misuse of power by executives to favor unrestricted authority. Boards can, of course, become a burden, interfering unduly in management, stifling creativity, seeing their function as one of control. Legally they are responsible. But the ideal is a partnership spirit in which the board exercises its trustee-ship with integrity and with a supportive, enabling attitude. Peter Drucker describes the relationship between board and executive officer well: "Their tasks are complementary. Thus each has to ask, 'What do I owe the other?' not 'What does the other one owe me?' The two have to work as one team of equals."

A key role of World Vision boards is to hold executive leaders accountable. These boards also need to be accountable, not only in a legal sense, but within the framework of commitments and relationships that are the basis of the World Vision Partnership. Over the years we have continued to work out how to achieve this in practice. We will continue to do so in the future, for relationships are never static. They change with situations and personalities.

I salute the men and women who serve on World Vision boards throughout the world. They give generously of their time and experience without payment or privilege, other than the fulfillment of serving Jesus Christ through World Vision. At critical times in our history they have had to make difficult decisions, accept heavy responsibility and stand with World Vision at great cost to themselves and their families.

MAKE THE ORGANIZATION MORE HUMAN

Jan Carlson, chief executive of Scandinavian Airlines System, devised a slogan for the 1980s as the airline stressed the importance of customer service at the point of contact. "Every person is a customer," went the slogan. In the 1990s he came up with a new slogan that took customer service to a deeper level, "Every customer is a person."

We mostly think of our history in terms of the organization: its personalities, its programs, budgets and events. But the real story is in the lives of people — donors and sponsors, as well as the people in project communities.

Years ago I went to the high, jungle-clad mountains of Irian Jaya (West New Guinea) to see our village training programs. Our small plane was dwarfed by the massive ridges as we looked for gaps between the peaks. "Impossible" landing strips cut into the sides of the mountains tested the skill of our pilot.

At the highland hub of Bokondini, World Vision had an exceptional training center led by Yonias Taedini. 'Nias, as he was known to his friends, was Timorese, but he had volunteered to work for World Vision among the primitive Dani people of the highlands. The project was one of the most successful I had ever seen; holistic development in the very best sense. I learned also that Nias had made an important contribution to the Dani church, bringing spiritual vitality and helping the people gain confidence in dealing with the authorities.

From Irian Jaya I went on to Perth, Australia, where I was to visit the recently established Perth office of World

Vision. I had been asked to speak to the staff about the "large picture." So I duly prepared my talk, reviewing what I considered key global strategies. When I arrived at the office, I found four chairs arranged in a little circle — one for each of the staff and one for me. Just as we were about to begin the phone rang. It was a sponsor with a question. I had lost a third of my audience!

I quietly folded up my prepared speech and shared from my heart some of the experiences that were fresh from my visit to Bokondini a few days earlier. It struck me that here was the essence of World Vision. Nias Taedini and these dear colleagues in Perth were the important people. They were the front line in our mission, and the people they served were the most important of all — the project communities and the donors. All the rest of us were facilitators helping to make the connections.

I come back to the theme of this chapter. We have looked at the organization from various perspectives. In our worst moments we may think all large organizations are hopeless. Yet they are also inevitable. People who leave one organization soon join or start another. The challenge is to make organizations more human for the people in them and those they serve. The work of organizational renewal is like painting the Sydney Harbor Bridge — it never stops!

Sometimes the tendency is to blame "the organization" for its faults, forgetting that those within organizations make them what they are. I am reminded of a comment made to me by Rev. Raymond Fung of Hong Kong. "Organizations always seem more sinful than the people in them." This brings us to the "people side" of World Vision, which we will now consider in more depth.

People of God, enabled by God and by each other; learning, talking, laughing, crying and sometimes even dying, working together in weakness and in strength to make a worthwhile difference....

— Carol Gray, World Vision United Kingdom

People Matter Most

"Death and violence are never far away. In the last three months:

- A staff member killed and three wounded in Angola.
- World Vision house bombed in Somalia, one person badly hurt.
- Mortar attack on World Vision base in Malanje, Angola.
- Colleague killed by bandits in Kenya.
- World Vision-supported clinic attacked by Khmer Rouge in Cambodia.
- Canadian colleague died of malaria in South Africa.
- International Office staff member murdered.
- Staff member killed by a land mine in Mozambique.

This is the cost of discipleship in hard currency."

So began my report to the World Vision International Board in March 1994. Most people see World Vision from a superficial external perspective. They may see it as some kind of big, impersonal machine. They do not have the opportunity of going behind the promotion or the general image they have of the organization, to the life and struggles of the people in it. No picture of World Vision would be adequate without this deeper encounter with its people, especially the price they pay for the sake of the mission.

Where Violence Lurks

On May 17, 1991, Jose Chuquin and Norman Tattersall arrived at World Vision's office in Lima, Peru. Jose had served as the national director in Colombia for 11 years. Norman, a Canadian, was a veteran with World Vision in Latin America and was at the time acting director in Peru. The two men were good friends as well as colleagues. They had come to the office to interview candidates for the position of national director in Peru.

As their car pulled up outside the office, the quietness of the morning was suddenly shattered. The air was filled by the deafening blast of machine-gun fire. A hail of bullets smashed into the car, leaving both men slumped in the back seat as blood poured from their wounds. They were rushed immediately to the nearest hospital where emergency surgery was performed.

Meanwhile, I had arrived at my office in California to begin the day's work. A few minutes later we received word of the attack. We informed the staff at once, asking everyone to pray, while we waited for further word. It wasn't long coming. My colleague David Tam came into my room.

"Norman has gone," said David simply.

I gathered the whole staff in our lunch room. We shared our grief with each other and with God. We prayed for Jose in his desperate fight for life. We prayed for the families of our colleagues and for the team in Peru. And we prayed for the assailants. We sensed our own fragile hold on life, yet affirmed together the love of God in Jesus Christ from which nothing can separate us. We sang the much-loved hymn, "Amazing Grace," and went back to our work as an act of dedication.

Jose Chuquin held on for eleven days by the miracle of medicine and a fierce will to live. But the damage to his body was too much in the end. Vice President Manfred Grellert was at Jose's bedside to help comfort his wife, Laura, as others of our team had gone to Norman's wife, Ivy, with the terrible news.

In a letter to me, Dr. Valdir Steuernagel of Brazil, a member of our International Board, wrote, "This is a painful hour for the World Vision family and for us in Latin America especially. It is very hard that the impoverishment experienced by most of our societies in Latin America embodies also a process where life becomes very cheap. How to rescue the sanctity of life in the midst of a society in decomposition is quite a challenge. But it must be faced in the name of Jesus."

A professional investigation could not confirm the reason for the murder of Norman and Jose, or the identities of those responsible. We have our suspicions, which must remain confidential in the interest of security. For most of us, even those who travel to dangerous places, this kind of violence seems to belong only in movies and novels. But in reality, evil always lurks in the shadows, especially where the servants of Jesus Christ work for change and justice among the poor. These two prominent leaders were not its only victims. In the same week four of our project workers in Peru disappeared, believed killed.

With great courage, Corina Villacorta of our Peruvian staff took charge immediately and continued to serve as director in the tense months that followed.

MIDNIGHT RENDEZVOUS

We learned in 1982 that the FMLN movement in El Salvador was broadcasting threats against World Vision staff, claiming that we were agents of U.S. foreign policy in the country. Through intermediaries in Mexico, we were able to arrange a meeting with FMLN leaders. Regional director Geoff Renner and I set off for Nicaragua, chosen as a neutral site for the meeting.

Late one night the small, serious group gathered in an obscure house in Managua. For three hours the deputy leader of the FMLN harangued us about the FMLN cause. We heard the well-known history of injustice against the peasant population of El Salvador and the accusation that World Vision was connected with forces of oppression, based mainly on the unfounded story coming out of Cambodia discussed in Chapter 8.

Geoff and I heard out the case until the speakers ran out of steam. Then it was our turn to speak. We described the way World Vision works in communities. I gave examples of our efforts for justice in several countries and the representations we had made to the United States Government from time to time on issues affecting the poor. The fact that Senator Mark Hatfield, a critic of U.S. policy in El Salvador, was a member of World Vision's U.S. board helped. I explained the newly-formed structure of World Vision International under the internationalization process.

Finally, Geoff and I offered to work in FMLN-held territory. It had always been our aim to serve poor communities on both sides of the conflict and here was a unique opportunity of speaking directly with the leaders.

We left the meeting feeling we had been heard and believed. The broadcasts did stop and gradually we were able to open up new work as promised. Here was another case of the critical importance of searching for points of connection and reconciliation with an apparent adversary, and in this case averting a possible tragedy.

More Guts Than Good Sense

"Hello, Jean," I said as Lebanon director Jean Bouchebl came on the line.

This was not a routine phone call. I was speaking from the podium of our International Office auditorium where the whole staff was gathered to hear the conversation, amplified over the sound system.

On the other end, Jean was in the midst of the daily shelling of Beirut. We could hear the explosions over the phone as we talked. He described the scene and the agony of this tortured city. We assured Jean of our prayers, our support and our love. We prayed for each other right there. Then we sang:

> Bind us together, Lord,
> Bind us together,
> With cords that cannot be broken.
> Bind us together, Lord,
> Bind us together,
> Bind us together with love.

We could not all stand with Jean Bouchebl in the shattered city. But we could enter into his experience in a way that drew our hearts together in solidarity. "Carry each other's burdens," wrote Paul, "and so you will fulfill the law of Christ" (Galatians 6:2).

World Vision's Beirut office took three direct hits during the war. Once during the night a shell exploded right outside the window of Jean's personal office. A piece of shrapnel tore a hole as big as a fist in the back of his chair.

"If this had happened two hours later, I would now be with God," Jean said.

In 1985 Jean, his wife Renee, and his two children were kidnapped. Taken from their car at a checkpoint, they were held in a cell where Jean was interrogated at gun point while his family was forced to look on. Later they were released unharmed.

"God's spirit kept us going," said Jean.

Right through the worst years of the war the staff would go out every day to the community projects to encourage the people and maintain the work.

In another dramatic event World Vision doctor Milton Amayun, nutritionist Rachael Singleton and two local staff were kidnapped in the West African country of Mali. They were on their way to a health care project in the remote seventh region where World Vision was assisting 100,000 nomadic people in the Sahara wilderness.

Sixty armed rebel bandits stopped the World Vision vehicle in the desert and accused the two foreigners of being journalists and spies.

"We are health workers," explained Milton in French, "and we are on our way to a project. We feed many of your children."

The group was unconvinced. On impulse, Milton took out his business card.

"You see I am a doctor," he said. "I work for World Vision. When you finish your revolution, get in touch with me. We could do a project together."

Immediately the atmosphere softened. The group took the vehicle and left the World Vision team in the desert without food or water. We learned later that the rebels used the vehicle in an attack on the regional capital of Menaka the same day.

Milton, Rachael and four others survived for six days and nights in the desert. They dug for dirty water in a dry river bed, sharing water with animals. They prayed for protection and, in Milton's words, "felt the Spirit of God embrace them."

They were saved when they met a man with two donkeys. "He was God's angel," said Milton. Eventually they reached a World Vision project site and safety.

The nature of World Vision's mission inevitably takes us to places of danger. An international leader once told me World Vision had "more guts than good sense." Yet we do not take these risks lightly or irresponsibly. The staff involved weigh up the dangers with their families. Special training is provided and procedures developed for emergencies.

THE INNER CIRCLE OF THOSE MOST DEAR

"Dad, we are your children too!", exclaimed my elder daughter Jo.

I had just returned from the Korean Children's Choir tour of Australia and New Zealand in 1971. It had taken me away from Fran and the children, ages 11 and 9, for three whole months. I came home full of what the choir members had done, where they had been, how they had behaved. No comparison was meant, no exclusion of my own dear children intended. But Jo's comment got my attention at once and made me think.

Many people have encouraged me to include in this book some words about the impact of World Vision and its ministry on personal and family life. This is difficult for two reasons. First, it would take a whole book to do justice to the subject. Secondly, these matters are intensely personal and private. Is it fair or wise to discuss them publicly? Yet, if people matter most, as I claim in this chapter, I need to consider how the organization affects those who matter most of all — my own family, for whom I have first responsibility.

I have described already the more extreme dangers faced by World Vision people in crisis areas. But there are other dangers too — subtle ones that often escape notice, yet are just as real. People engaged in Christian service tend to equate their Christian duty with their professional job. In other words, their job or the organization is seen as their "work for God," while the family is something else. In an attempt to address this danger, some will try to establish a simplistic order of priorities — "God first, family second, work third" — as if God could be put in an insulated box. God is in all of life; our families, friendships, recreation, our private moments, as well as our work.

As a practical matter, when you are a person engaged in work centered on caring for others, motivated by a sense of Christian duty and frequently absent from home you have the ingredients for depriving your family of their legitimate and necessary share of your life. This is not what you intend. You desire with all your heart to be a good father, a good mother, a loving husband or wife. But consciously or unconsciously you expect your family to understand the claims of others on your life. And mostly they do, often in heroic measure.

My younger daughter, Ros, has worked with me closely over several months as I have written this story. When I started to think about including a family section, she offered to write about her experience. Here it is in her own words:

FROM THE VIEWPOINT OF A WORLD VISION KID

I am Graeme's younger daughter, Ros. For 27 of my 33 years World Vision has been part of my family. I guess you could say I'm a "World Vision kid," like other children in this book whose lives have been impacted by World Vision. I was six years old when I first heard the words "World Vision," the organization that took our family to Melbourne where Dad was the first Australian director. When I was 13 World Vision meant a move to Los Angeles, California, where I attended high school and university. Now, as an adult, I've chosen to live again in Australia. But World Vision follows me still. My parents' visits are short and bittersweet, governed by itineraries determined by World Vision.

Writing this story is not easy. For in my story, World Vision is a benefactor — providing food, shelter, clothes, education, travel, moments of fame; and a thief — taking away time, attention, feelings, identity, life. I usually avoid even talking about World Vision because many of my feelings are tangled up with a taboo that says, "World Vision does such wonderful work. How can you complain about it when it's helping people who don't have food?" So for me it's just easier not to say anything about it.

But then I think about the story Dad tells in this book of World Vision's journey as an organization, and I am reminded how it has moved from the recognition of basic human needs to include recognition of basic human rights. World Vision saw that it was not enough to provide food, shelter, and clothing; that people needed other things — like freedom, safety, dignity, a future — and that the human spirit and indeed the body sometimes die for lack of these things. I'm glad World Vision believes that God wants the human family to have life and live it to the full. But I cannot believe it's right for World Vision to deny this same life to its own families. So, I'll take a deep breath and lift the lid off the pot....

As you may well imagine, seeing people in need and being involved in meeting that need has a powerful impact on those who participate in these opportunities for service. For World Vision staff members, this work changes their lives. In some cases it can take over their lives and consume the lives of their families as well. Working for World Vision can put family loyalties in conflict, leaving many World Vision staffers fighting hard to leave work at the office in order to have a "normal" home life.

Like any kid, I wanted to say to my father, "I'm angry (or sad) that you're leaving again. I don't want you to go. I need you here." Because there's always a crisis somewhere else that takes Dad's attention, I ended up thinking, "I'm not very important in the scheme of things." But how could I express those feelings when my father might be flying to Vietnam to save other children's lives? Their need seemed so much greater than mine. So perfectly normal feelings and fears are pushed down. Wanting something for yourself seems selfish. Soon you feel guilty for having anything when other children have nothing.

While I learned early to "be strong," in other ways I felt ill-equipped. World Vision had opened my heart to the world outside, but where did I find the skills to survive the world of the high-school campus where they seemed to speak a different language? This was the world I had to deal with. Another of the feelings I buried was anger, the kind that gives the strength to survive, the will to fight back, the belief that things should be different and the energy to do something to change them. I think kids can cope with knowing that the world doesn't always fit what they want. Certainly this is something we all have to learn sooner or later. But learning this is somehow more bearable when one is able to protest.

My father's constant traveling and involvement with World Vision's work in dangerous situations fueled my childhood fears that he might not come back. A couple of years ago, Dad was traveling from Europe to the East Coast of the U.S. to join my mother and sister for Christmas. A delay caused him to take a later flight than he had intended. Watching the news that night, he saw the terrible images of the Lockerbie wreckage. Stunned, he said, "I could have been on that flight!" This fear of losing someone you love transfers to other relationships too.

Because we lived during my growing-up years far from extended family, friends and a familiar culture, our immediate family became very close and and dependent on one another. Being together as a family has been our security. Now as adults and physically separated as a family, I think my sister and I have found it harder to make our own lives, harder for our parents to let go.

Returning to Australia felt like the start of my life. I hoped to find out who I was apart from my parents and out from under the shadow of World Vision. But it's not been that easy. Finding my own life has been more than just moving back to a place that said "home." It also became an inner journey opening up the home inside to those musty, ugly feelings I'd shoved in the back room. I've disliked travel because of anxiety attacks. Now that I'm finding my inner home base, it is becoming easier to leave a familiar framework because I now know who I am wherever I am.

Over the years I think Dad has become more aware of the family's needs and has committed himself more and more intentionally to fulfilling his role in our family as well as World Vision. I appreciate his efforts now to let us know we come first, encouraging us to phone at any time, even if it means interrupting a meeting.

Being able to be ourselves when we are together and keeping a sense of humor has helped our family cope with being in the light of Dad's leadership role in World Vision. Being able to talk and laugh about silly things — like the time Dad lost his balance in running down a slope at home and bumped his head on a tree trunk — helps to keep us, and him, aware that we're all human and real underneath the skin.

Many of us want to hide the fact that we're not perfect people; that family members and family life are not perfect. Leaders are especially vulnerable, because people expect them to be different. Yet we all need freedom to share sorrows as well as triumphs with brothers and sisters in Christ, who came to set us free. Living under the public's gaze and expectations can lock us into silence and pain, adding pressure on those already living with the world's pain.

I'd like to see the World Vision of the 21st century caring for its staff in specific ways, beginning with not asking so much of them under the banner of Christian ministry that their families lose out. I'd like to see World Vision as a supportive, global network of families exchanging books, tapes, personal news, a World Vision kids club, Parent Effectiveness Training courses, a library and resource persons for encouraging families. Caring about and for family life may be another step along the road in World Vision's journey as an organization.

Obviously there are personal costs in being involved with the work of World Vision. Nothing worthwhile is without cost. Sometimes I think the cost of a parent's involvement is borne mostly by the family, while the benefits go to other children and other families. Despite the cost, I'm glad Dad chose to work in the area of helping people. I admire him for it, and others like him.

Mine is a fierce sense of justice. I hate the cruelty and suffering I see in the world. I want to believe that the world benefits from each life World Vision touches — the children, women and men who are alive but would not have been and who are free to live normal, everyday lives full of challenge and contentment, joy and sorrow. I want to think that in the end — as my mother says, quoting Julian of Norwich — "All will be well. All manner of things will be well."

"And I heard a loud voice from the throne saying, 'Now the dwelling of God is with men, and he will live with them. They will be his people, and God himself will be with them, and be their God. He will wipe every tear from their eyes. There will be no more death or mourning or crying or pain, for the old order of things has passed away.' He who was seated on the throne said, 'I am making everything new!'" (Revelation 21:3-4)

Many families, not only in World Vision, but in similar organizations, churches and missions may share these experiences. If organizations are to become more human, we who are responsible for them will have to work more seriously at easing the pressure on families. Probably we need additional help from professionals — and a great deal of determination to make it happen. I must confess that, as president of World Vision International, I have not done what I could and should have done to help families understand and cope with these pressures. This failure is one of my great regrets.

LEARNING TO COPE WITH SUFFERING

"How do you manage to cope with seeing so much suffering?"

I have been asked this question countless times. The encounter with suffering is always painful and difficult. Emotions of anger, grief, despair and futility surge in upon the senses like pounding waves that never stop. And those waves leave their mark, just as the ocean carves the shore. None of us can remain untouched by suffering. We learn to cope with it by doing what we can whenever we can, to ease or eliminate it.

For me, coping starts by trying to understand how suffering calls forth the depth and breadth of God's love. I am not asked to take the burden of suffering on myself. Nor am I to blame God for the existence of suffering. The roots of suffering lie in humanity's estrangement from God and it is the divine intent that life should be recreated through faith and wholeness. Thus I become a participant in God's encounter with suffering. Together with all who enter into the afflictions of others, I am a point of connection with a healing presence far beyond my own — the limitless love of God.

I am constantly inspired by the courage I find among people in the midst of suffering. In Mozambique two years ago I had the privilege of honoring Pastor Simao Agusto, who maintained a caring ministry in RENAMO-held territory throughout the worst years of the Mozambique war. He and his wife were held captive for three years during this period. Amid the horrors of this brutal war he formed and sustained 40 small churches, encouraging the people in their grief and suffering, supporting himself and his family by doing carpentry. With no formal education, he brought over 4,000 people to faith in Jesus Christ.

At a joyful celebration of worship in the northern city of Quelimane, I paid tribute to Simao Agusto and his wife. People had come from all the churches in the region to celebrate the coming of peace to Mozambique and to honor the pastor. They sang, they danced, they gave thanks to God. Then, on behalf of all the churches, Pastor Agusto presented me with a communion flask and six goblets, fashioned simply by hand from ebony wood.

For me that communion set was a symbol of hope. I was to be in Somalia within two days and promised the congregation that we would use the communion set as a sign of encouragement to others still in the midst of their agony. "In this way we will all be drawn together in a fellowship of suffering," I said. "You will give your sisters and brothers a message of hope."

Later that week in Baidoa we gathered at dawn for communion. I arranged the flask and goblets in the center of our little group and explained their significance. Charles Clayton, executive director of World Vision United Kingdom, was there. He recalls the moment:

We gathered in a small room which had open slats in the brickwork, so that the sounds of the early morning marketplace were coming through. We each took a tiny drop of wine. A piece of bread was broken. We reminded ourselves of the words of Jesus, which were very poignant in this land of broken bodies and spilled blood. We prayed for personal forgiveness and national healing as children's voices drifted through the openings in the wall, and we remembered our Lord.

The "fellowship of suffering" keeps me from yielding to despair. How can I give up and walk away, when I have looked into the eyes of Simao Agusto and his wife?

Night.
Across nations — turbulent darkness.
Before the dawn — a dream.
A dream of a new World Vision
Coming into being in community,
Somewhere, far and still.
North and South, East and West
Reaching out
To cry and laugh,
To listen and challenge,
To struggle and search
Together
In God;
No longer just to feed the world,
But to heal the world,
So that the world can feed itself
In fraternal justice.

— Frances O'Gorman

15

The Road Ahead

As I write these words I feel like a hiker who has reached a hilltop on a long trail. I look back and see the distance covered over the 28 years of my journey with World Vision, with its twists and turns, its peaks and valleys. But this is not merely an individual, personal journey. It is an organizational journey, a journey together.

I began my story by referring to three tracks or paths. The vision path starts off at the signpost "Compassion and Evangelism." That's the general direction of the path for the whole journey, but the landscape changes as the path goes on. The early landscape is called social welfare — orphanages, baby homes, clinics and hospitals. The path moves on to developing self-reliance, and later to empowerment as we begin to understand how poor communities can work together for change. We recognize some of the things that keep people poor and see the need for justice.

Along the way we care for the casualties in ever larger numbers through emergency relief. Throughout the journey we try to follow our guide, Jesus Christ, who knows the path and helps us explain it to others. I suspect that in some foggy patches we may lose sight of him at times and do not always understand his directions.

There is another path running beside the vision path like an access road, secondary but necessary. It is called the organizational path. There are two kinds of travelers on this path: those who have the supplies and those who need them. At first the pioneer, Bob Pierce, obtains the supplies and dispenses them. But soon there is more work than he can manage and he needs help. Other suppliers join the effort and form a kind of partnership. The partnership eventually extends to all the travelers, who realize they are on the same journey and need each other's help if they are to make the destination.

My view of the journey focuses on our enlarging vision and growing understanding of mission. And it indicates changes in the shape of the organization needed to support the mission. You have seen this interplay between vision and structure throughout the book. I have said earlier that these transitions are not as simple as they sound. They have been debated, prayed over, experimented with over time. They do not imply judgment on the past or arrogance about the present, but rather a process of learning in which all have been involved. The main problem is keeping the organization in step with vision. It tends to lag behind and sometimes hinder the vision rather than support it.

Then there is my personal pathway interweaving the journey. I have described the journey as I have seen it. I have been influenced by the vision and the organization and have had a hand in their shape and direction. A growing multitude of companions have been on the journey with me, like the participants in one of those great marathon races where thousands join in along the way. Many who read this book may already be part of that great company of people who strive to do the best things in the worst times.

KEEP MARCHING OFF THE MAP

In his last address to a World Vision audience three months before his death in June 1991, former president Stan Mooneyham told a story to illustrate World Vision's journey. The story concerned the days when map-making was a rudimentary science because so much of the world was unexplored and unknown. The map-makers represented the area outside of their knowledge with symbols of dragons, monsters and big fish. This uncharted territory was seen as dangerous, terrifying and, if possible, to be avoided.

Stan's story was about one adventurous commander of a battalion of Roman soldiers who found himself in that unmapped territory. He did not want to turn back, but neither did he want to pursue his course without further instruction. So he dispatched a messenger to Rome with the urgent request, "Please send new orders. We have marched off the map!"

Stan Mooneyham compared World Vision's story with the adventurous spirit of that Roman commander — creating new ideas, going to difficult places, attempting the untried. He challenged us to "keep marching off the map!"

Now as we look toward a new century there will be unmapped territory ahead in terms of the social, political, economic and religious context in which we work. We do not know the kinds of dragons we may meet, though on today's sophisticated information highway we have access to tools and knowledge that help us forecast some of the conditions we are likely to encounter. But however well we prepare, as we must, the element of uncertainty remains.

One of my Scottish namesakes, Andrew Irvine, was a famous Himalayan climber. With George Mallory he pioneered the early routes on Mt. Everest, almost reaching the summit before his death on the mountain in 1924. When asked why he faced such danger, Mallory said, "The greatest danger in life is not taking the adventure."

World Vision will continue to take the adventure. The vision will keep expanding, the organization will keep changing, the company of people will keep growing and learning. My companions on the journey so far and those yet to join the path will take us into the future. They will stand on tiptoe to see the dawn of the new century and go on into the fullness of its day. I look forward to reading about their adventure!

CHANGING A PARADIGM

As I turn from the trail behind me and see it rise toward the distant heights ahead, I can discern something of its direction. To some extent the way has already been mapped out, based on where we have come from.

For example, when I visited Korea soon after I had been given responsibility for our field operations in 1975, I met with the board of directors for World Vision Korea, still chaired then by Dr. Han Kyung Chik. I reminded the board that World Vision's ministry had been pioneered in Korea — childcare, emergency relief, leadership development, evangelistic outreach. "It would be fitting," I said, "for Korea to pioneer a new direction — the transition from a field to a support country."

And so it was. A shift in emphasis began. The Korean churches already had a missionary vision for Asia and beyond. Now it was time for World Vision to capture that same vision. It started with sponsors of Korean children being recruited in Korea itself. At first this meant that fewer resources were needed from abroad for Korea. These resources could therefore be released for work elsewhere. Gradually Korean donors reached beyond their own country to assist others.

Today Korea has become a major donor country. Hong Kong and Taiwan have made the same transition. In fact, the old paradigm of "giving" and "receiving" countries (or field and support countries) is rapidly and deliberately disappearing in World Vision. Jerry Chang, executive director of World Vision Taiwan, writes of his experience:

The most significant transformation I have witnessed in my six years with World Vision is in World Vision Taiwan itself. In 1988 the focus of our work was primarily the rural indigenous people in the country. Our budget was totally contributed from abroad and the staff as a whole was content with what was happening.

Realizing the strength of Taiwan's economy was on the rise, it became clear that we should no longer rely on funds from abroad. However, the normal status quo mentality had to be overcome. Furthermore, the task of fund-raising was new to most of the staff. We began our transformation with a few who were convinced of its importance.

By 1992 we were totally self-reliant. Today we help finance projects in over 60 countries. Of course the real gain cannot be measured in dollars and cents. Instead of looking inward only to the problems of Taiwan, the staff now see the whole world as our market place. Our life perspective has changed.

Our ministry in Taiwan has both broadened and deepened. Apart from rural development, urban ministry has become an important focus. We run a toll-free 24-hour hotline network for child abuse. Also we cooperate closely with churches in social services. People in Taiwan now have the opportunity to realize the blessings of giving.

People and communities are being transformed in other parts of the world because of our contributions and prayers.

As Jerry indicates, this change is not only about money. It has more to do with human dignity and the common life we share on this planet. We are moving beyond a traditional philanthropy of the rich giving to the poor. Most of World Vision's donors are not rich, and some of the most generous are those who have least. World Vision's vice president for Africa, James Mageria, put it well when he said, "None are so poor that they have nothing to give; none so rich that they have no need to receive."

I am not suggesting that people should cease to give. I do want to put it in the light of a larger vision, a mature understanding of what it will take to live as one people, sharing who we are as well as what we have.

This vision is extending through Asia. In 1995 most World Vision countries in Asia took part in a "30-Hour Famine," typically a program run by World Vision in affluent countries. Thirty thousand people took part in places as distant as Bangladesh and Papua-New Guinea. By fasting for 30 hours and asking friends to donate so much per hour for their fast, these people identified with others whose plight they knew from their own experience. It was a new dimension of caring for many. It moves us toward the beautiful picture given by Paul to the Christians at Corinth, "...there should be no division in the body, but its parts should have equal concern for each other. If one part suffers, every part suffers with it; if one part is honored, every part rejoices with it" (1 Cor. 12:25,26).

The new direction is taking hold in Latin America, where Vice President Manfred Grellert and his colleagues have a strategic vision to move away from dependency and be part of a larger world view. Economist David Befus has introduced well-founded small credit programs designed to sustain development with poor communities, a form of solidarity economics. With assistance from Peter McNee, former executive director of World Vision New Zealand, a new mind set is emerging that looks toward releasing resources within Latin America, not only among the rich, but all people.

Even in Africa, with its enormous needs, a new vision is emerging. In Tanzania, for example, one rural community studied World Vision's Mission Statement in depth. They concluded that they wanted to be more fully part of the total mission. They began supporting their project with their own cash gifts and now contribute over one third of the project budget. They took seriously the part of the Mission Statement that calls for "Public Awareness — that leads to informed understanding, giving, involvement and prayer."

Aggrey Kassano of World Vision Tanzania sees this change as a "process of reversal." He writes:

The process has oriented communities to be responsible for their own development when World Vision funding phases out and the community takes over. This is focusing on gradually making the programs community-based, sustainable, highly integrated and transformational.

From Ethiopia's abyss of suffering in the 1980s, the same exciting vision comes through in the words of former World Vision director Yemane Michael:

World Vision Ethiopia is always changing. The staff have started to sponsor children. Is this not a big attitudinal change? At this pace, I think after a short time we will hear that World Vision is funding the program in its country and most probably in the neighboring countries!

TOWARD A NEW GLOBAL VISION

Globalization is a modern phenomenon. We have a global marketplace, global communications and increasingly a global economy. But it is not enough to see frontiers disappear for trade, news, entertainment, information or finance. Globalization motivated by competition for profit or advantage will only multiply the forces that produce poverty and injustice. We need a new global vision of our common humanity and our shared responsibility for life on this planet.

Richard Falk describes globalization driven by market, financial and technological forces as an imposed globalization-from-above. He suggests that globalization-from-below in the form of trans-national networks and democratic social forces can provide a necessary balance that benefits all people. Some refer to this globalization-from-below as an emergent civil society, in which non-governmental organizations like World Vision play an important part.

In an article titled The Birth of the Global Nation, Strobe Talbott describes the forerunner of the nation-state as "a prehistoric band clustered around a fire beside a river in a valley. Its members had a language, a set of beliefs and a repertoire of legends about their ancestors. Eventually they forged primitive weapons and set off over the mountain, mumbling phrases that could loosely be translated as having something to do with 'vital national interests' and 'manifest destiny.' When they reached the next valley, they massacred and enslaved some weaker band of people they found clustered around some smaller fire and thus became the world's first imperialists."[1]

Talbott goes on to describe the formation of empires, which were more or less in a constant state of war. Eventually the empires yielded once more to the nation-state. Many enlightened minds over the centuries saw both the need and the possibility of a larger view of humankind, in which interests higher than those of the nation were given primacy.

"Humanity has discovered, through much trial and error," writes Talbott, "that difference need not divide." He points to the modern phenomenon of the sharing of power upward through supranational bodies, outward toward commonwealths and common markets, and downward through the empowerment of people. He concludes his article by envisioning a day when "we won't really be so very far from those much earlier ancestors, the ones huddled around that primeval fire beside the river; it's just that by then the whole world will be our valley."[2]

Russian poet, Yevgeny Yevtushenko wrote, "Nations are losing their ability to hear each other's heartbeats. Many international negotiations break down because they are built

1. *The Independent* newspaper, London, November 24, 1993.
2. *The Independent* newspaper, London, November 24, 1993.

on mutual accusation instead of mutual confession." Here is a call for a different globalization that takes us from merely contemplating the sufferings of others to sharing them.

In 1967, philosopher Bertrand Russell wrote in his own handwriting a final review of his life and work. He concluded his last testament with these words:

> Consider for a moment what our planet is and what it might be. At present, for most, there is toil and hunger, constant danger, more hatred than love. There could be a happy world, where cooperation was more in evidence than competition, where what is lovely in nature was not destroyed to make room for hideous machines whose sole business is to kill, and where to promote joy is more respected than to produce mountains of corpses. Do not say this is impossible: it is not. It waits only for people to desire it more than the infliction of torture. There is an artist imprisoned in each one of us. Let him loose to spread joy everywhere.[3]

Let him or her loose! Russell signalled what has become the most dramatic social development in human society in the second half of this century. That is, the collective power of people to take charge of their own destiny and shape their own future. In the last fifty years we have seen empires crumble, dictators fall and oppressive systems removed by the actions of people whose spirits would not be crushed.

HOLDING ON TO THE DREAM

In the darkest days of Nicolai Ceaucescu's brutal dictatorship in Romania, Pavel Chirila and his wife Mia,

3. Time, July 20, 1992.

both doctors, carried on a dangerous and compassionate ministry among the regime's oppressed people, many of them traumatized by torture. Their patients included those considered worthless under the state ideology.

A small group of friends met one night in a room at the Cernica Orthodox Monastery near Bucharest to formulate their dream for a Christian medical association that would operate a hospital with a holistic approach to health care, conduct research and train nurses. They called it the Christiana Medical Association. One of their group, a Roman Catholic priest, was later imprisoned. While in prison he shared the dream with his cell-mate, who encouraged him to hold on to the dream. "The worst defeat," he said, "is for someone to take away your dream."

After Ceaucescu's fall, Pavel and Mia Chirila fulfilled the dream; Christiana became a reality. In 1992 Fran and I had the joy of visiting the hospital. Dr. Chirila has brought together Orthodox, Roman Catholic and Protestant Christians to care for the poor and the sick. Fran and I were touched by the integrated approach to healing evident in the hospital. We were inspired by the eagerness of the nurse trainees, many of them young nuns, in their crisp white uniforms. We saw the pioneering work being done by Mia's research unit. In less than six years Christiana has built a network of over 2,000 medical professionals.

On a later visit I laid the foundation stone for the interconfessional chapel that will be the core of a new building for the hospital. The same night Pavel and Mia Chirila invited a group of friends and associates to gather for dinner in the same room at the Cernica Monastery where the dream was born. Reflecting on his experience, Dr.

Chirila said, "Christianity has a holy rule; in each physical or moral trial there is the possibility of a spiritual leap."

Whether our vision is the sweeping vista of a caring, responsible global society, or the close-up vision of a broken life restored, the vital ingredient is the same — undiminished hope. Without it, the road ahead leads to a dead end.

Pavel and Mia Chirila did "the best things in the worst times, and hoped them in the most calamitous." They held on to the dream. They sustained hope in the midst of darkness. They believed that however dark the night, the dawn would come. You cannot hold back the dawn.

Our premise: To live together with misery and injustice and to continue to have hope.

— *Regina Longa, World Vision Brazil*

 *Epilogue*

Tipping The Scales Toward Life

O
ver the years Fran and I have enjoyed reading books together. Her serious sight impairment in earlier years made reading painful for her. So we would choose a book, usually a novel, which I would read aloud. The tales of the great Scottish storyteller, John Buchan, were among our favorites.

In my work, I have found that life is not like a novel, yet the noble ideas of these stories stay with me. One in particular inspired me.

It is 1938. Sir Edward Leathen, a prominent British barrister and one-time attorney general, discovers he has cancer and can expect to live no more than a year or two. Despite his distinguished career, he feels a strange emptiness, a feeling that he has not contributed significantly to life. Something is missing; a cause, a giving of himself to some noble aim.

While brooding over these matters, Leathen receives a call for help from his niece in New York. Her husband, a French Canadian, has disappeared on a mysterious quest into the vast white North of Canada. Leathen sets off to find him.

The search leads Leathen and his native guides deep into the great wilderness, where they are caught by the approaching winter. Eventually they find the missing man, lost and mentally confused. They begin the long, agonizing journey back on foot, through the frozen wastes. All the time Leathen's energy is waning as his condition deteriorates.

The party reaches a remote settlement where a tribe of Hare Indians is fighting a losing battle for survival. Sickness has ravaged them and they are dying out. Only a Roman Catholic priest, Father Duplessis, remains with the Hares. Leathen also receives the news that Britain has declared war on Hitler's Germany. He feels weak and depressed. A sense of futility sweeps over him. Here he is dying in a lonely backwater, his dream of doing something useful unrealized, while the world plunges into yet another conflict. In this melancholy mood, Leathen sinks into a fitful sleep. We take up the story as Buchan told it...

Leathen awoke with a far off tinkle in his ears. Father Duplessis in his little church was ringing the morning Angelus.

That tinny bell had an explosive effect on Leathen's mind. This was a place of death, the whole world was full of death — and yet here was one man who stood stubbornly for life. Here was one man, at any rate, who was the champion of life against death.

The world was at war again. It might be a twilight of the gods, the end of all things. The globe might swim in blood. Death might resume his ancient reign. But, by Heaven! he would strike his blow for life, even a pitiful flicker of it.

There was a plain task before him, to fight with Death. God for his own purpose had loosed it in the world, ravaging over places which had once been rich in innocent life. Here in the North, life had always been on sufferance, its pale, slender shoots fighting a hard battle against Elder Ice. But it had maintained its brave defiance.... And now one such pathetic slip of life was on the verge of extinction. This handful of Hares had for generations been a little enclave of life besieged by mortality. Now it was perishing, hurrying to share in the dissolution which was overtaking the world.

By God's grace that should not happen — the God who was the God of the living. Through strange circuits he had come to that simple, forthright duty for which he had always longed. In that duty he must make his soul.

There was a ring of happiness in his voice. "You have me as a helper," he said.[1]

To strive to do the best things in the worst times is to have a vision of hope. It is to back life's scent against its stench. It is a belief in the capacity of the human spirit to discover a better way and above all, to yield to the transforming work of Jesus Christ, not "once upon a time," but

1. Buchan, John. *Mountain Meadow.* New York: Literary Guild of America, 1940.

day in and day out. I have seen this spirit of hope in the darkest corners of the earth.

The process of transformation must continue in all of us, the affluent, the poor, the institutions we create. And it must start with me, where I am. One thoughtful, caring act contributes more to a better world than a hundred theories merely talked about. This may sound simplistic and naive, but it is what I learn from Jesus as I read the records of his life and seek to know his presence.

You may feel overwhelmed by the course of events. You are only one person. Anything you could do for a better world would be a mere drop in the ocean, a grain of sand on an endless shore. But even a single grain helps tip the scales toward life. Do not fret about whether it counts or not. Let him look after that who said, "I have come that they may have life and have it to the full." He is the source of all life, even Jesus Christ, our Lord. And he says to us, as he did to those simple fishermen by the lakeside, "Come, follow me."

Let him hear us say, "You have me as a helper!"

Appendix A

Chronology

50s

CRITICAL EVENTS

- 1950 - World Vision founded. Incorporation papers signed. Office opened in Portland, Oregon, U.S.A.
- 1953 - Child sponsorship program started.
- 1953 - First pastors' conference in Korea.
- 1954 - World Vision Korea office opened
- 1955 - World Vision logo designed
- 1956 - Office moved to Los Angeles
- 1957 - First issue of World Vision magazine
- 1957 - World Vision office opened in Canada

MINISTRY FOCUS

Founded by Bob Pierce, World Vision set its course to "care for the fatherless and widows, to help the poor and starving, to care for the sick and to seek to present the gospel of Jesus Christ." When the Korean War ended in 1953, World Vision began its child sponsorship programs to support orphanages and widows' homes. Bob Pierce gathered 300 Korean church leaders for the first pastors' conference. The objectives and ethos of World Vision formed during these pioneering years.

ORGANIZATIONAL FOCUS

At end of 1959:

- Countries with World Vision offices. 3
- Projects 165
- Children in program 13,215
- Annual operating budget. . . . . .US$2.7M
  (excluding gifts-in-kind)

PRINCIPLE FUNDING SOURCES

- Church engagements
- Meetings and conventions

PRESIDENT

Bob Pierce 1950 to 1967

60s

CRITICAL EVENTS

- 1961 - Korean Orphan Choir first tour
- 1961 - Evangelistic outreach in Tokyo
- 1965 - World Vision headquarters moved from Pasadena to Monrovia, California
- 1966 - MARC program began
- 1966 - World Vision Australia office opened
- 1967 - Bob Pierce resigned

MINISTRY FOCUS

Relief and rehabilitation work began. Ministry expanded beyond orphans and widows to others in need. Korean Orphan Choir formed. Missions Advanced Research and Communications Center (MARC) began in association with Fuller Theological Seminary. Evangelistic crusades in Tokyo and Osaka. Major response to war victims in Vietnam. Transition from pioneering era to "second generation" of ministry.

ORGANIZATIONAL GROWTH

At end of 1969:

- Countries with World Vision offices 9
- Projects 388
- Children in program 32,600
- Annual operating budget. . . . . .US$5.1M
  (excluding gifts-in-kind)

PRINCIPLE FUNDING SOURCES

- Church film screenings
- Radio audiences
- Direct mail
- Conventions
- Space advertising

PRESIDENTS

Bob Pierce until 1967
Stan Mooneyham from 1969

70s

CRITICAL EVENTS

- 1971 - World Vision New Zealand office opened
- 1972 - First television special
- 1973 - Love Loaf program started
- 1974 - World Vision objectives changed to include "Developing Self-Reliance"
- 1974 - First office in Africa (Kenya)
- 1975 - Closure and evacuation in Indochina
- 1975 - First office in Latin America opened (Colombia)
- 1975 - World Vision office started in Europe (based in Germany)
- 1977 - Regional offices opened in Africa, Latin America and Asia
- 1978 - Internationalization process completed
- 1978 - Operation "Seasweep"
- 1978 - Training for all development staff at IIRR, Philippines
- 1979 - Dr. Bob Pierce died at age 64
- 1979 - Cambodia program re-established

MINISTRY FOCUS

Emergency relief expanded, with emphasis on world hunger. Television outreach launched. Evangelistic campaigns held in Indonesia and Cambodia. Community development introduced as major new direction. World Vision forced to close programs in Vietnam, Laos and Cambodia. Fifty orphan babies evacuated. "Operation Seasweep" rescued refugees from South China Sea and made international statement about plight of boat people. The 100th pastors' conference held at Taegu, Korea.

Development approach to child sponsor-funded programs adopted in 1979. World Vision committed to integrated, holistic approach to ministry.

ORGANIZATIONAL GROWTH
At end of 1979:
- Countries with World Vision Offices 40
- Projects 1,932
- Children in program 214,525
- Annual operating budget . . . . US$38.1M
  (excluding gifts-in-kind)

PRINCIPLE FUNDING SOURCES
- Television
- Government grants (mainly USAID)
- Direct mail
- Love Loaf
- Church film screenings
- Radio programs and spots
- Space advertising
- News media
- World Vision publications
- Volunteers (especially Australia and New Zealand)

PRESIDENT
Stan Mooneyham 1969 to 1982

80s

CRITICAL EVENTS

- 1980 - Middle East office opened
- 1982 - Hong Kong and Singapore support offices started
- 1983 - "Together" magazine began
- 1984 - Catastrophic famine in Ethiopia
- 1984 - Major relief in Mozambique and Sudan
- 1986 - Bylaws changed to achieve balance of field and support office delegates at World Vision International Council
- 1986 - Large scale development introduced
- 1987 - Child survival programs started
- 1987 - Geneva office opened
- 1987 - World Vision Japan support office opened
- 1988 - Programs began in China
- 1989 - Core Values adopted

MINISTRY FOCUS

Africa became focus as massive famine hit Ethiopia, bringing unprecedented public response worldwide. Civil war in Mozambique and Sudan added to drought disaster. World Vision mounted Africa-wide response, with main focus on Ethiopia. Response included large food distribution programs. Large scale development, mainly for water resources and three-year child survival campaign launched. Health programs started in China, with emphasis on women and children. Fresh focus on empowerment of urban poor through Office of Urban Advance. European and Asian support ministry established.

ORGANIZATIONAL GROWTH

At end of 1989:
- Countries with World Vision offices. 55
- Projects 5,509
- Children in program 833,583
- Annual operating budget . . . . . . .US$153.6M
  (excluding gifts-in-kind)

PRINCIPLE FUNDING SOURCES

- TV specials, news stories, advertising
- 30/40 Hour Famine programs
- Various government grants
- Love Loaf
- Major donors
- World Vision publications
- News media
- Direct mail
- Performing artists
- Radio
- Volunteers

PRESIDENTS

Ted Engstrom 1982 to 1984
Tom Houston 1984 to 1988
Graeme Irvine 1989 to 1995

90s
CRITICAL EVENTS

- 1990 - Major overhaul of sponsorship program
- 1990 - Advocacy for justice intensified
- 1990 - One million sponsored children
- 1991 - Stan Mooneyham died at age 66
- 1992 - Womens' Commission proposals adopted
- 1992 - New Mission Statement adopted
- 1993 - Somalia emergency response
- 1994 - World Vision response to Rwanda catastrophe
- 1994 - Children of War program launched
- 1995 - Covenant of Partnership ratified by all member countries
- 1995 - Christian Witness Commission recommendations adopted
- 1995 - Task Force brings changes in World Vision governance and structure

MINISTRY FOCUS

Collapse of European communism enabled World Vision to expand in many former Soviet-bloc countries. Increased focus on advocacy for justice took World Vision into global arena on issues of Cambodia, Palestinian rights, land mines, child exploitation, girl child initiative and arms trade. Sponsorship-funded development concentrated in larger area programs. Major relief efforts included crises in Somalia and Rwanda and other emergencies on every continent. Commitment to public awareness and fund raising extended to all World Vision countries, while response to inner-city poor and emergencies in affluent countries increased.

ORGANIZATIONAL GROWTH

At end of 1995:

- Countries with World Vision offices. 74
- Projects 5,049
- Children in program 1,082,952
- Annual operating budget . . . . US$269M
  (excluding gifts-in-kind)

PRINCIPLE FUNDING SOURCES

- Substantial government grants
- TV outreach
- Major donors
- Special events
- World Vision publications
- 30/40 Hour Famine
- Performing artists
- Love Loaf
- Radio advertising and interviews
- News media
- Regional media networks
- Direct mail

PRESIDENT

Graeme Irvine 1989 to 1995

Appendix B

A Statement Of Core Values For World Vision International

As the World Vision Partnership has grown to encompass over sixty national entities, we have recognized a need to strengthen the sense of common understanding that binds us together as a ministering community. We have identified certain values that lie at the centre of this understanding. These we have termed "Core Values" and we define them as fundamental principles that determine our actions.

These values are fashioned from our experience in ministry. They express the ethos of World Vision as we understand it and the essential character to which we yet aspire as an organization. We state them in the present tense, not because we have attained them, but so that we may hold them alongside our actions as a constant challenge. We confess how often and how far we have fallen short. We commit ourselves, by the grace of God, to press toward this expression of a preferred future.

OUR CORE VALUES

We are Christian. We acknowledge one God; Father, Son and Holy Spirit. In Jesus Christ the love, mercy and grace of God are made known to us and all people. From this overflowing abundance of God's love we find our call to ministry.

We proclaim together, "Jesus lived, died and rose again. Jesus is Lord." We desire him to be central in our individual and corporate life.

We seek to follow him — in his identification with the poor, the powerless, the afflicted, the oppressed, the marginalized; in his special concern for children; in his respect for the dignity bestowed by God on women equally with men; in his challenge to unjust attitudes and systems; in his call to share resources with each other; in his love for all people without discrimination or conditions; in his offer of new life through faith in him. From him we derive our holistic understanding of the gospel of the Kingdom of God, which forms the basis of our response to human need.

We hear his call to servanthood and see the example of his life. We commit ourselves to a servant spirit permeating the organization. We know this means facing honestly our own pride, sin and failure.

We bear witness to the redemption offered only through faith in Jesus Christ. The staff we engage are equipped by belief and practice to bear this witness. We will maintain our identity as Christian, while being sensitive to the diverse contexts in which we express that identity.

We Are Committed To The Poor. We are called to serve the neediest people of the earth; to relieve their suffering and to promote the transformation of their condition of life.

We stand in solidarity in a common search for justice. We seek to understand the situation of the poor and work alongside them toward fullness of life. We share our discovery of eternal hope in Jesus Christ.

We seek to facilitate an engagement between the poor and the affluent that opens both to transformation. We respect the poor as active participants, not passive recipients, in this relationship. They are people from whom others may learn and receive, as well as give. The need for transformation is common to all. Together we share a quest for justice, peace, reconciliation and healing in a broken world.

We Value People. We regard all people as created and loved by God. We give priority to people before money, structure, systems and other institutional machinery. We act in ways that respect the dignity, uniqueness and intrinsic worth of every person — the poor, the donors, our staff and their families, boards and volunteers. We celebrate the richness of diversity in human personality, culture and contribution.

We practice a participative, open, enabling style in working relationships. We encourage the professional, personal and spiritual development of our staff.

We Are Stewards. The resources at our disposal are not our own. They are a sacred trust from God through donors on behalf of the poor. We are faithful to the purpose for which those resources are given and manage them in a manner that brings maximum benefit to the poor.

We speak and act honestly. We are open and factual in our dealings with donor constituencies, project communities, governments, the public at large and with each other. We endeavor to convey a public image conforming to reality. We strive for consistency between what we say and what we do.

We demand of ourselves high standards of professional competence and accept the need to be accountable through appropriate structures for achieving these standards. We share our experience and knowledge with others where it can assist them.

We are stewards of God's creation. We care for the earth and act in ways that will restore and protect the environment. We ensure that our development activities are ecologically sound.

We Are Partners. We are members of an international World Vision partnership that transcends legal, structural and cultural boundaries. We accept the obligations of joint participation, shared goals and mutual accountability that true partnership requires. We affirm our inter-dependence and our willingness to yield autonomy as necessary for the common good. We commit ourselves to know, understand and love each other.

We are partners with the poor and with donors in a shared ministry. We affirm and promote unity in the Body of Christ. We pursue relationships with all churches and desire mutual participation in ministry. We seek to contribute to the holistic mission of the church.

We maintain a cooperative stance and a spirit of openness toward other humanitarian organizations. We are willing to receive and consider honest opinions from others about our work.

We Are Responsive. We are responsive to life-threatening emergencies where our involvement is needed and appropriate. We are willing to take intelligent risks and act quickly. We do this from a foundation of experience and sensitivity to what the situation requires. We also recognize that even in the midst of crisis, the destitute have a contribution to make from their experience.

We are responsive in a different sense where deep-seated and often complex economic and social deprivation calls for sustainable, long-term development. We maintain the commitments necessary for this to occur.

We are responsive to new and unusual opportunities. We encourage innovation, creativity and flexibility. We maintain an attitude of learning, reflection and discovery in order to grow in understanding and skill.

OUR COMMITMENT

We recognize that values cannot be legislated; they must be lived. No document can substitute for the attitudes, decisions and actions that make up the fabric of our life and work.

Therefore, we covenant with each other, before God, to do our utmost individually and as corporate entities within the World Vision Partnership to uphold these Core Values, to honor them in our decisions, to express them in our relationships and to act consistently with them wherever World Vision is at work.

Signed this 22nd day of September, 1989 by the participants in the fifth World Vision International Council.

Appendix C

WORLD VISION is an international partnership of Christians whose mission is

to follow our Lord and Saviour Jesus Christ
in working with the poor and oppressed
to promote human transformation,
seek justice and bear witness
to the good news of the Kingdom of God

WE PURSUE THIS MISSION through integrated, holistic commitment to

Transformational Development

that is community-based and sustainable, focused especially on the needs of children;

Emergency Relief

that assists people afflicted by conflict or disaster;

Promotion of Justice

that seeks to change unjust structures affecting the poor among whom we work;

Strategic Initiatives

that serve the Church in the fulfilment of its mission;

Public Awareness

that leads to informed understanding, giving, involvement and prayer;

Witness to Jesus Christ

by life, deed, word and sign that encourages people to respond to the Gospel.

WORLD VISION INTERNATIONAL

Appendix D

A Covenant Of Partnership

INTRODUCTION

In 1978 the boards of the several "incorporating members" of an enlarged and restructured World Vision International met "to be launched by the Holy Spirit upon a new venture in partnership and ministry"(Declaration of Internationalization, 31st May, 1978). Under the guiding, correcting and enlightening influence of the same Holy Spirit we have seen the Partnership so launched extend to encompass over sixty national entities.

Our corporate pilgrimage has brought us to new understandings of relationship and ministry. Sensing the need to express these shared understandings as a framework for joint global action, a Covenant of Partnership has been formulated. The Covenant is based on the principle of inter-dependent national entities held together, under God, by voluntary commitment rather than legal contract. On this basis the national entities are envisaged as functioning in a complementary, cohesive manner in which national interests are recognized, but are regarded as secondary to the larger whole. We affirm the spirit of citizenship in the Kingdom of God described in Ephesians; "... fellow-citizens with God's people and members of God's household, built on the foundation laid by the apostles and prophets, with Christ Jesus himself as the foundation-stone" (Ephesians 2:19,20).

ELEMENTS OF PARTNERSHIP DEFINED

The World Vision Partnership refers to the entire World Vision family throughout the world. Any expression of the World Vision ministry is in some way connected to the Partnership. The word "Partnership" is used in this document in a broad, informal sense, rather than a legal sense.

World Vision National Entities comprise the membership of the Partnership. The conditions and categories of membership are described in the bylaws of World Vision International. All function with the guidance and advice of a National Board or Advisory Council.

World Vision International is the registered legal entity that, through its Council and Board of Directors, provides the formal international structure for the Partnership.

The World Vision International Council provides the membership structure for the Partnership. It meets every three years to review the purpose and objectives of World Vision, assess the extent to which they have been accomplished and make recommendations to the World Vision International Board in relation to policy. All member-entities are represented on the Council.

The World Vision International Board of Directors is the governing body of World Vision International as outlined in the bylaws. The membership of the Board is broadly representative of the Partnership and is appointed by a process determined by the Partnership.

The International Office is the functional unit of World Vision International housing most of the central elements of World Vision International. It operates under the authority of the World Vision International Board of Directors.

THE COVENANT

Regarding World Vision as a partnership of interdependent national entities,

Affirming the principle of relationships based on commonly held mission, values and commitments,

Acknowledging the process of internationalization that has brought the World Vision Partnership to its present stage of development, and

Recognizing the need for a statement of the rights and obligations of member entities,

We, as a properly constituted national World Vision Board (or Advisory Council), do covenant with other World Vision Boards (or Advisory Councils) to:

A. Uphold the following statements of World Vision identity and purpose:
   1. The Statement of Faith, that declares our shared beliefs as Christians, as members of many churches.
   2. The Mission Statement, setting out the fundamental purpose and activities of World Vision.
   3. The Core Values, which emphasize our commitment to Jesus Christ and the poor, and describe the character to which we aspire as an organization.
B. Contribute to the enrichment of partnership life and unity, by:
   1. Sharing in strategic decision-making and policy formulation through consultation and mechanisms that offer all members an appropriate voice in Partnership affairs.

2. Communicating clearly to constituencies and the public that we are members of a larger, international Christian Partnership.

3. Accepting the leadership and organizational structures established by the World Vision International Council and Board for the operation of the Partnership.

4. Carrying out World Vision ministries in a manner that is sensitive and responsive to national cultures and contexts.

5. Observing and practicing at all levels a modest lifestyle as reflected in buildings and furnishings, compensation levels, class of travel and accommodations and general mode of operation.

6. Engaging in direct, open dialogue with other entities on issues of tension or conflict, seeking constructive solutions that seem best for all concerned and demonstrating the power of reconciliation in Christ.

7. Fostering an open spirit of exchange for ideas, proposals, vision and concern within the Partnership.

8. Encouraging board members and staff in their participation in the worship and life of a local church, which is important to our Christian existence and a sign of our corporate commitment to support the Church in her global mission.

C. Work within the accountability structures by which the partnership function, by:

1. Affirming the principle of mutual accountability and transparency between all entities,

including our willingness to have our ministries (including domestic ministries) and our financial affairs evaluated and examined and our compensation programs reviewed, with due notice, by appropriate Partnership representatives.

2. Accepting Partnership policies and decisions established by World Vision International Board consultative processes.

3. Honoring commitments to adopted budgets to the utmost extent possible.

4. Ensuring that where Partnership entities plan bilateral arrangements that are outside already agreed Partnership plans, World Vision International is consulted, in agreement and regularly informed.

5. Consulting with World Vision International or other member entities on decisions that may have a significant impact on other members of the Partnership.

6. Executing an agreement with World Vision International to protect the trademark, name and symbols of World Vision worldwide.

7. Ensuring that we establish no office or program outside our own national borders without the consent of both World Vision International and the host country.

D. Observe agreed financial principles and procedures, especially:

1. Using funds raised under the auspices of World Vision exclusively in World Vision approved ministries.

2. Keeping overhead and fund raising expenses to a minimum to ensure that a substantial majority of the funds raised are responsibly utilized in ministry among the poor.
3. Remitting through World Vision International all resources intended for ministry outside of donor countries, with the exception of direct project funding under approved bilateral agreements.
4. Accepting the Financial Planning and Budgeting Principles adopted by the World Vision International Board as the framework for Partnership financial operations.
5. Ensuring that funds or commodities accepted from governments or multilateral agencies do not compromise World Vision's mission or core values, and that such resources do not become the major ongoing source of support.

E. Present consistent communications messages, that:
1. Reflect our Christian identity in appropriate ways.
2. Include words, images, numbers and statistics that are consistent with ministry realities.
3. Avoid paternalism and cultural insensitivity.
4. Are free from demeaning and degrading images.
5. Build openness, confidence, knowledge and trust within the Partnership.

In signing the Covenant, we are mindful of the rich heritage of Christian service represented by World Vision and of the privilege that is ours to join with others of like mind in the work of the Kingdom of God throughout the world.

We therefore recognize that consistent failure to honor this Covenant of Partnership may provide cause for review of our status as a member of the Partnership by the Board of World Vision International.

Signed in behalf of (name of national entity)

by resolution carried at a meeting of the (Board or Advisory Council) on_____

Chair of (Board or Advisory Council)

For Further Information

World Vision is a partnership of more than 65 national entities working together in a shared task in more than 100 countries of the world. Most of these national offices have their own national boards, trustees or advisory councils.

World Vision International is constituted separately from any of the national entities to coordinate the global operations of the Partnership and represent it in the international arena.

Established in 1950 to help children orphaned in the Korean war, World Vision has over the intervening years broadened its objectives, extended its scope and become truly international in its character and structure. World Vision's Mission Statement (see appendix C, page 277) explains what we are all about.

If you would like to contribute to World Vision International or learn more about its world-wide ministry please contact us at:

World Vision International
121 E. Huntington Drive
Monrovia, California 91016

To order additional copies of

Best Things In The Worst Times

Please send _____ copies at $15.00 for each trade paperback book and/or _____ copies at $22.00 for each hard cover book, plus $3.50 shipping and handling for each book.

Enclosed is my check or money order of $_____
or [ ] Visa [ ] MasterCard
#_____ Exp. Date ____/____
Signature _____

Name _____
Street Address _____
City _____
State _____ Zip _____
Phone _____

(Advise if recipient and shipping address are different from above.)

For credit card orders call:
1-800-895-7323

or

Return this order form to:

BookPartners
P.O. Box 922
Wilsonville, OR 97070